MW01713393

Not just Another JOURNAL

CAPTAINS & POETS

blah
blah
blah

Copyright © 2022 Captains & Poets
All rights reserved.

No part of this book may be reproduced in any form or used in any manner without written permission of the copyright owner except for the use of brief quotations in a book review.

First paperback edition February 2022

Version 1.0
ISBN Canada 978-1-7775099-5-8 (Paper)

Published by Captains & Poets
www.captainsandpoets.com

this book belongs to

write your name using a font and colours that show who you are!

ME

before you get started

Sit back, chill,
watch this movie

www.captainsandpoets.com/video

Rate it!

☆ ☆ ☆ ☆ ☆

"I wish I had known about this when I was younger."

– The Daily News

"This movie will change your life!"

– That Hollywood Guy

What did you think?

Who did you relate to?

What are your favourite Captain and Poet traits?

welcome

Use this journal in your own way.
Here are some tips to get started:

Journal every day or once in a while when you need it.

Do these ones around the dinner table.

Jump around or go page by page.

Pick a page with your favourite number on it and start there. 13! 88! 123!

Use your Poet to get in touch with your creativity and what matters most to you.

When you need a boost call on your Captain to get you into action!

And remember to have fun along the way!

SNACK
something to snack on
something to mark up pages
something to hydrate
your favourite playlist
something to stick stuff
something to cut up stuff
something for thinking, imagining and creating
something to look up the authors of the cool quotes in here
some stuff you might need

Meet the Poet

Poet barometer

How is your Poet today?

How does your Poet measure a good day?
What has to happen?

the Poet is in EVERYONE

Everyone has a Poet inside but they show up a little differently for everyone. Which quote from the Poets in the video did you relate to the most?

- ☐ "They help me by being able to empathize with others, being able to empathize with myself and just being able to be in touch with my own emotions."
- ☐ "my Poet acts as a compass in my life because it guides me to what I truly want to do and what makes me happy...really trusting my gut almost."
- ☐ "my Poet helps me with my friendships and my relationships with people. I wouldn't be able to understand people as much as I can now."
- ☐ "I would say that my Poet shows up in my life by my moral compass and my desire to help others."
- ☐ "my Poet likes reading and writing fiction and fantasy. It increases my imagination and that helps me make sense of anything."
- ☐ "my Poet is the thing inside of me a thousand layers deep, your internal instinct."
- ☐ "The Poet is who you are before the filter."
- ☐ "If I'm a car, my Poet is the gas...It's the thing that you constantly need to add to keep going."
- ☐ "The Poet is the characteristics that form a good leader... because being a good leader, it's not about commanding people or telling them what to do, it's about supporting them."

How would you describe the Poet in your own words?

who are you?

Underline the words that describe your Poet.
Circle the words that you want to be more of.
Draw a picture of your fabulous Poet!

EMPATHETIC
CARING
ARTISTIC
CREATIVE
DREAMER
KIND
SENSITIVE
IMAGINATIVE

OBSERVANT
PERCEPTIVE
INTUITIVE
REFLECTIVE
WISE
LISTENS WELL
SOULFUL
PASSIONATE

How much of a POET have you been lately?

- [ ] Created something awesome
- [ ] Noticed something no one else did
- [ ] Expressed my feelings
- [ ] Sensed something going on around me
- [ ] Followed my gut
- [ ] Imagined a new way of doing things
- [ ] Felt what someone else was feeling
- [ ]

→ Give yourself a point for each answer. Add them up and check your score!

Poet in waiting 1–2 Points

The world is missing out on knowing who you are. Spend some time getting to know yourself better and then ask your Captain to help you take steps to put yourself out there more.

Poet on the rise! 3–5 Points

Great job practicing sharing your Poet with the world! Now take it a step further by picking one item from the list above to work on.

A natural Poet! 6–7 Points

Woot woot! Your Poet is a big part of who you are. Imagine how being your BEST Poet will help you be the best person you can be and take it to the next level!

A master Poet! 8 Points

Wow! Your Poet is thriving! Keep up the great work and when you have an off day try something from the list to help you get back in the zone! Don't leave your Captain behind!

Dear Poet

The best part about being a Poet is...

This helps me know who I am because...

Dear Poet

The hardest part about being a Poet is...

I am going to work on this by...

Dear Poet

One thing I like about you is...

One question I have about you is...

You remind me that all of the answers are inside of us.
I have a feeling the answer to this question is...

First thing my poet thinks about in the **MORNING**

Last thing my poet thinks about at **NIGHT**

my passionate Poet

The Poet is more obvious in some people than others but they are always there driving your passions.

Are you the kind of person who has a quiet passion or do you wear it on your sleeve so everyone knows?

What are you passionate about when it comes to: sports, books, friends, food, life? Write down whatever comes to mind!

my Poet playlist

Songs that inspire the Poet in me.

Poet maze

Figuring out who you are is a journey inward...

And just when you figure something out, there is something new to discover! The journey never ends...

would you rather?

Be a river	or	Be an ocean
Shower 5x a day	or	Brush your teeth 20x a day
Celebrate a lifetime of birthdays on one day	or	Celebrate your birthday every day for one year
Be a TikTok sensation	or	Be an actor in a popular tv show
Internet down	or	Laryngitis
Be a horse that flies	or	Be a bird that gallops
Listen to music with earplugs	or	Watch tv blindfolded
Be a famous author	or	Be the character in your favourite book
One best friend	or	100 acquaintances
See long distance	or	Have microscopic vision
Read a book backwards	or	Listen to an album backwards
French fries dipped in chocolate	or	Pizza covered in icing

If you made a poet **TIME CAPSULE** at this stage of your life, what would be in it?

How would you like your poet to be described when people open it?

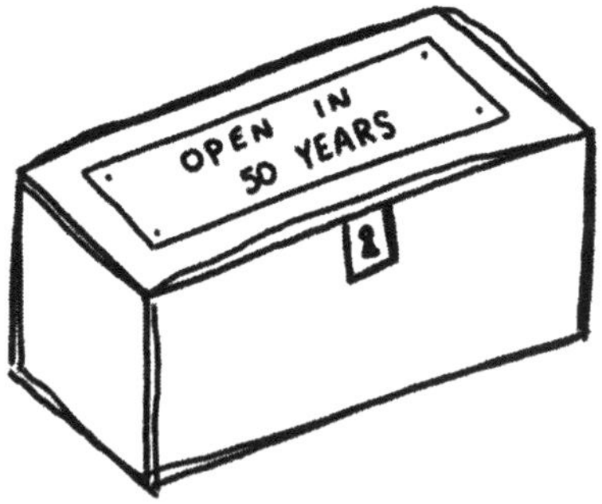

mindfulness exercise

→ Name **5** things you can see.

→ Name **4** things you can smell.

→ Name **3** things you can hear.

→ Name **2** things you can touch.

→ Name **1** thing you can taste.

What did you notice just happened to you when you did that? Hhhhmm. mindfulness...

where art & science meet

Pick up something from nature. Draw it here or paste a photo of it on this page.

What is cool about its design?

What do you notice about it that you didn't notice before?

What does it remind you of?

How are you like this object?

"Look deep into nature, and then you will understand everything better."

– Albert Einstein

favourite smell

favourite sound

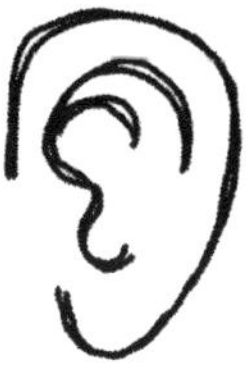

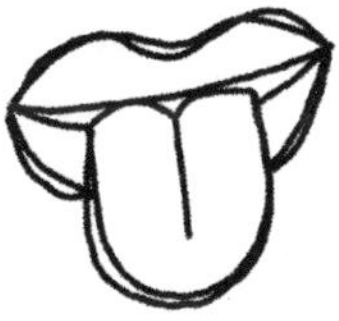

favourite taste

favourite sight

what my poet wishes for the **WORLD**

"You don't create your mission in life – you detect it."

–Viktor Frankl

Poet texts

If your Poet could text you throughout the day what would you want them to say?

What would the notification sound like?

Dear Poet

Today was a great day! Thanks for being there like when...

Dear Poet

Today was a hard day. I need your help...

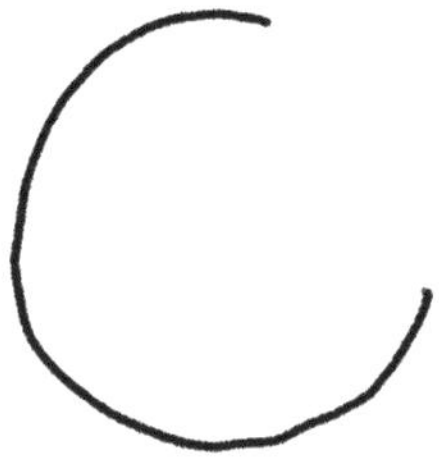

doodle starters

Connect the doodles to draw a picture. Add your own doodles too!

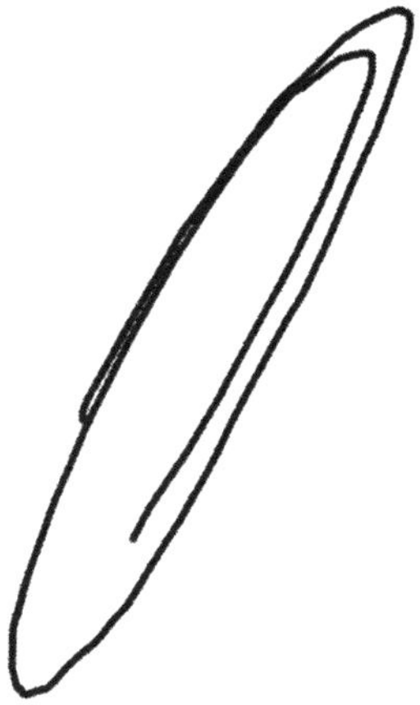

most **CREATIVE** idea you have ever had!

Doodle it into reality!

my favourite word →

→ What is it about it you love? The sound, the meaning, the feeling you get when you say it? Describe it using more favourite words!

everyone has a BOOK inside them

Read the first and last sentence of a book.
Fill in what happens in between using
experiences and characters from your life...

first sentence:

who?
what?
where?
when?
why?
how?

last sentence:

Send your WORRIES to the CLOUDS
(and let them go)

Sometimes we just need to acknowledge what is worrying us and then we can set it free. Write down the three things that are worrying you the most right now. What would your life be like without those worries? Imagine them floating away...

Poet conversation starters

Did you see something beautiful or interesting today?

What did you imagine today?

How did you feel today?

What did you notice today?

What did you create today?

What was the best thing that happened today?

When did you wish your Poet had shown up today?

When did your Poet show up today?

most **OUTRAGEOUS** idea you have ever had!

Doodle it into reality!

"The visionary starts with a clean sheet of paper, and re-imagines the world."

– Malcolm Gladwell

"Those who don't believe in magic will never find it."

– Roald Dahl

make believe is make believe

The world is full of magic if you look for it. Recall something "magical" you believed in or imagined as a child and sketch a picture of it here so you can hold onto it. When was the last time you experienced something magical?

haiku philosophy

Life isn't always neat and tidy like a rhyming poem. But putting it into a poem can help. Haiku means "starting verse" so it is a good way to start expressing your thoughts about something. Create Haikus to express life as you know it these days.

Captain and Poet (5 syllables)
Pulling me back, forth, back, forth. (7 syllables)
Telling me "be me!" (5 syllables)

Life is a highway
Leading me to somewhere new
With no directions

When the sun shines down
Everything feels okay
I look up and smile

mindfulness exercise

Pick up an object, any object you see.

Look at it up close.

What is it's texture, smell, taste? (only if it's edible!)

What do you notice about this object that you never noticed before?

How does this object remind you of you?

What did you notice just happened to you when you did that? Hhhhmm. mindfulness...

Sometimes we just need to find a way to get it all out.

scribble all over this page

(like you're in Kindergarten again!)

word scramble

Unscramble as many Poet words as you can. Good luck!

crvatiee ____________________

etpamhetic ____________________

atiistrc ____________________

mavaetigini ____________________

revltefcie ____________________

oesrbvtan ____________________

utietiinv ____________________

dnesartunndgi ____________________

MANDALA

A mandala's pattern helps us focus and colouring them can help us process emotions. Colour this amazing mandala design and see how it takes you somewhere new. Hhhhmm. mindfulness.

the colour of my Poet

Close your eyes and imagine a situation where your Poet is feeling great – calm, creative and at peace with the world.

What colour would you use to describe your Poet right now?

Fill in the circle with that colour.

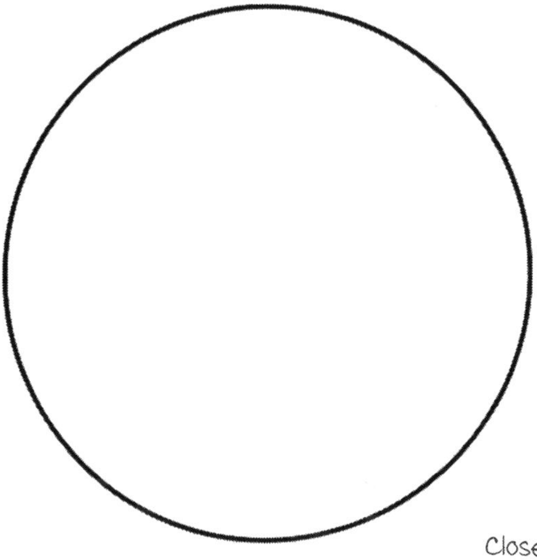

Come back to this page when you are feeling a bit off inside or need to release some tension.

Close your eyes and imagine you are breathing in the colour you chose and that it spreads all over your body, especially to the parts that aren't feeling so great.

Exhale slowly.

Repeat this process until you are feeling more like yourself again. Hhhhmm. mindfulness.

Poet Scavenger Hunt

Find objects that remind you of your Poet, trace or draw them on the page. Or put them in a box for safekeeping!

Something that...

- [ ] is your favourite belonging
- [ ] you love to read
- [ ] is your favourite colour
- [ ] makes you feel happy
- [ ] reminds you of home
- [ ] is quirky and only you appreciate
- [ ] smells good to you
- [ ] is gooey
- [ ] is fragile
- [ ] makes you smile
- [ ] inspires your creativity
- [ ] inspires you
- [ ]

Read this whole page with a straight face.

Read it silently.

Don't wiggle your ears. Don't flare your nostrils.

Don't smile.

Don't look away.

Don't say a word. Don't move your lips.

Read this next part in your best suspicious voice.

Who is that knocking at the door?

Now read **THIS** sentence in your best dramatic voice.

NOW YELL THE WORDS IN THIS SENTENCE IN YOUR HEAD. SCREAM ABOUT ALL THE THINGS THAT DROVE YOU CRAZY TODAY. SILENTLY.

Now close your eyes and forget about the world.
Oh wait, then you can't read.

Who is the part of you doing this?

Is that your Poet?

Who is the part of you watching you do this?

Is that your Poet?

Now you can smile.

Poet yoga poses

Yoga reminds us to listen to our body and pay attention to how we are feeling. Try a few yoga poses and hold them for a little while. Remember to breathe deeply and only do what feels good. Don't forget to switch sides for Balancing Half moon.

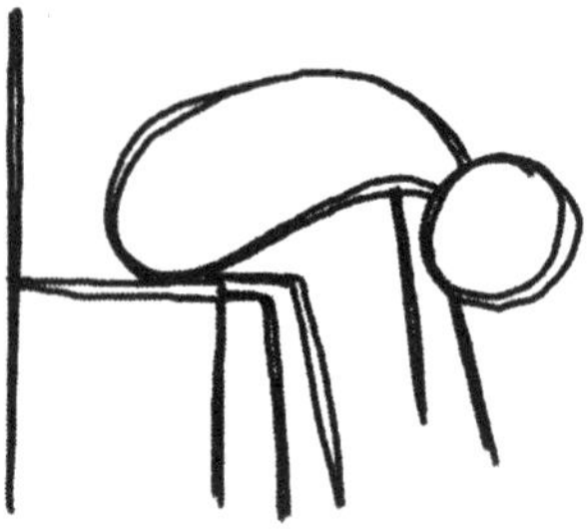

Wheel

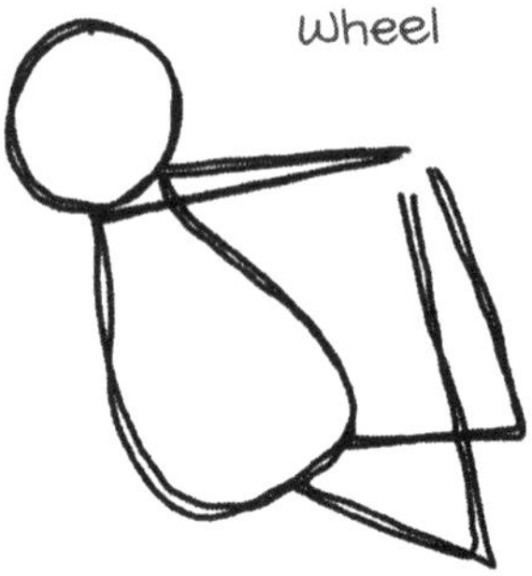

Forward Bend
(Try it standng to)

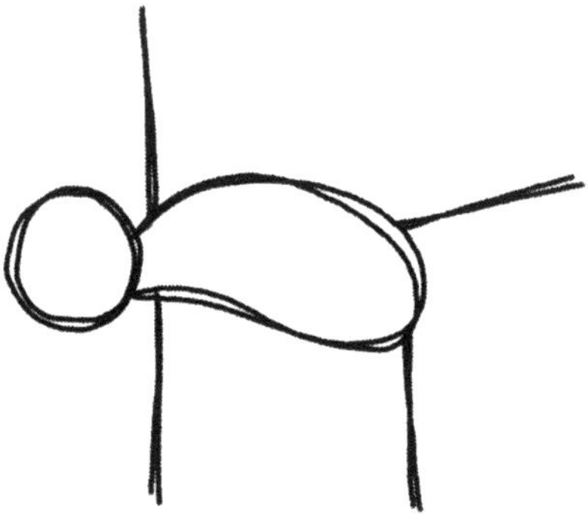

Bow

Balancing
Half moon

Rabbit

Use these poses whenever you need to get in the Poet zone.

A Poet's vision

The Poet is like an architect of the world. Close your eyes and imagine the ideal world you want to create to live in. Draw it or describe it below. Now go to page 82 and your Captain will help you bring it to life.

"If my mind can conceive it and my heart can believe it – then I can achieve it."

– Muhammad Ali

in the of blink an EYE

Imagine if every time we blinked we got a photo that was added to an album of our life. Next time you are having a moment you want to remember, take a snapshot and collect a few of them here.

"All that we see or seem is but a dream within a dream."

– Edgar Allan Poe

Poet daily self - assessment

How much of a Poet were you today?

Creative	1	2	3	4	5
Artistic	1	2	3	4	5
Empathetic	1	2	3	4	5
Imaginative	1	2	3	4	5
Reflective	1	2	3	4	5
Perceptive	1	2	3	4	5
Listens well	1	2	3	4	5
Caring	1	2	3	4	5
Kind	1	2	3	4	5
Observant	1	2	3	4	5
Sensitive	1	2	3	4	5
Intuitive	1	2	3	4	5
Understanding	1	2	3	4	5

an AFFIRMATION a day keeps the blues away

Circle the affirmation that is most valuable for you today. Say it three times and repeat it throughout the day! Find an image that represents what it means to you and put it in this page as a bookmark for when you need reminding!

Everything always works out.

my heart is open.

my voice matters.

Poet Crossword

Watch the video and look for the answers to these questions in this Journal!

Down

1. My Poet is what gives me a unique perspective on the world.

5. My Poet gives me the ability to explore my ______.

6. My Poet ______ me of what is important to me.

Across

2. My Poet is what ______ me to others' Poets.

3. My Poet shows me what my ______ are so I can explore them with the help of the Captain.

4. My Poet loves to ______ everything from art to friendships.

7. My Poet sees the ______ in the world.

ANSWERS: PERSPECTIVE, EMOTIONS, REMINDS, CONNECTS, GIFTS, CREATE, MAGIC

POET "QUOTES"

"make each day your masterpiece."

– John Wooden

"We are like islands in the sea, separate on the surface but connected in the deep."

– William James

"Try to be a rainbow in someone's cloud."

– Maya Angelou

"Yesterday I was clever, so I wanted to change the world. Today I am wise, so I am changing myself."

– Rumi

"Who looks outside, dreams; who looks inside, awakes."

– Carl Jung

"Beauty is not in the face; beauty is a light in the heart."

– Kahlil Gibran

"The only journey is the one within."

– Rainer Maria Rilke

"Worry is a misuse of the imagination."

– Dan Zadra

"The quieter you become, the more you can hear."

– Ram Dass

"You are the sky. Everything else is just the weather."

– Pema Chodron

"There is no greater agony than bearing an untold story inside you."

– Maya Angelou

Meet the Captain

Captain barometer

How is your Captain today?

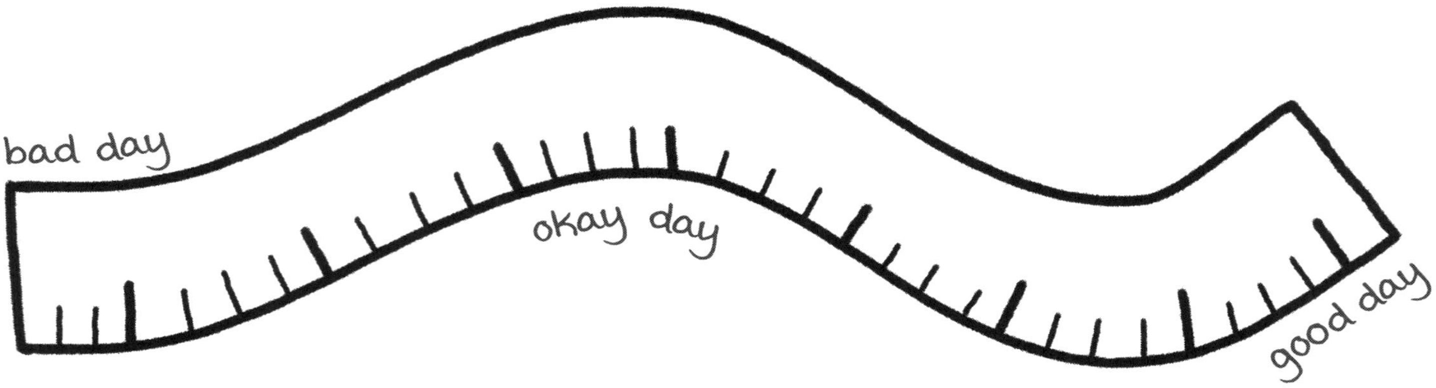

How does your measure a good day?
What has to happen?

the Captain is in EVERYONE

Everyone has a Captain inside but they show up a little differently for everyone. Which quote from the Captains in the video did you relate to the most?

- [ ] "my Captain uses past experiences to help me make better decisions in the future and make sure I'm happy along the way."

- [ ] "my Captain is the guy who takes risks, the guy who's always out there for the team in sports, video games, etc. my Captain's the more competitive side of me."

- [ ] "I lead with my Captain a lot... because I've needed to get out of my comfort zone kind of meeting new people or doing new things."

- [ ] "If I knew about my Captain earlier, I think I wouldn't be as introverted as a child. I would be not as shy and be super open to meeting new people and trying new things."

- [ ] "When you're learning to play an instrument...with the Captain helping you with that, it's easier to do it for longer."

- [ ] "Over the years my Captain has grown. It's helped me to know how to stand up for people."

- [ ] "...your Captain is the part of you that helps to show who you are."

- [ ] "...my Captain would be my wheels, the thing that actually takes me somewhere – the boldness, the actual actions that you take is your Captain."

How would you describe the Captain in your own words?

who are you?

Underline the words that describe your Captain.
Circle the words that you want to be more of.
Draw a picture of your fabulous Captain!

DECISIVE

ADVENTUROUS

HARD WORKING

AMBITIOUS

HELPFUL

CONFIDENT

BOLD

FOCUSED

PRACTICAL

DETERMINED

ORGANIZED

ASSERTIVE

ACTION-ORIENTED

TAKES CHARGE

GOAL ORIENTED

How much of a CAPTAIN have you been lately?

- [ ] Tried something new
- [ ] Set or achieved a goal
- [ ] Helped someone out when they needed it
- [ ] Learned from experience
- [ ] Went on an adventure
- [ ] Got out of my comfort zone in a good way
- [ ] Was bold and shared a part of myself with the world
- [ ]

→ **Give yourself a point for each answer. Add them up and check your score!**

Captain on the bench 1–2 Points

The world is missing out on seeing you in action. Spend some time exploring what you like to do. If you aren't sure where to start ask your Poet to remind you of what matters most to you.

Captain on the rise! 3–5 Points

Great job practicing sharing your Captain with the world! Now take it a step further by picking one item from the list above to work on.

A natural Captain 6–7 Points

Woot woot! Your Captain is a big part of who you are. Imagine how being your BEST Captain will help you be the best person you can be and take it to the next level!

A soaring Captain! 8 Points

Wow! Your Captain is thriving! Keep up the great work and when you have an off day try something from the list to help you get back in the zone! Don't leave your Poet behind!

Captain's log

Dear Captain,
The best part of being a Captain is...

This helps me know who I am because...

Captain's log

Dear Captain,
The hardest part about being a Captain is...

I am going to work on this by...

Captain's log

One thing I like about you is...

One question I have about you is...

You remind me that I can work through any problem.
I need you the most when...

Your Captain loves to

get things done

It feels good to get on top of things. make a list and check each item off. Then give yourself a reward.

my Captain playlist

Songs that inspire the Captain in me.

Captain maze

Figuring out who you want to be is a quest...

And just when you reach your destination, there is something new to discover! The journey never ends...

would you rather?

Wear your cltohes inside out	or	Wear your clothes backwards
Travel to the past	or	Travel to the future
Go camping	or	Stay in a hotel
Roller Coaster	or	Waterslide
Live in the clouds	or	Live in an underwater Kingdom
Climb Mount Everest	or	Dive seven leagues under the sea
Run everywhere you go	or	Walk backwards everywhere you go
A piercing on your toe	or	A tattoo of your toe
Go to bed at midnight and wake up at noon each day	or	Go to bed at noon and wake up at midnight each night
Travel to other planets	or	Travel to the centre of the earth
Live in medieval times	or	Live in the jurassic era
Bionic arms	or	Bionic legs

If you made a captain **TIME CAPSULE** at this stage of your life, what would be in it?

How would you like your Captain to be described when people open it?

mindfulness exercise

Notice what position your body is in right now. Is it open? Is it strong? Shift to a Captain position. What do you notice about how you feel?

Draw the before and after here.

What did you notice just happened to you when you did that? Hhhhmm. mindfulness...

travel wish list

"Wherever you go becomes a part of you somehow."

– Anita Desai

1.

2.

3.

Captain's log

Dear Captain,
Today was a great day! Thanks for being there like when...

Captain's log

Dear Captain,
Today was a hard day. I need your help...

Life is an adventure

What is the next adventure you would like to take?

How do you make everyday life an adventure?

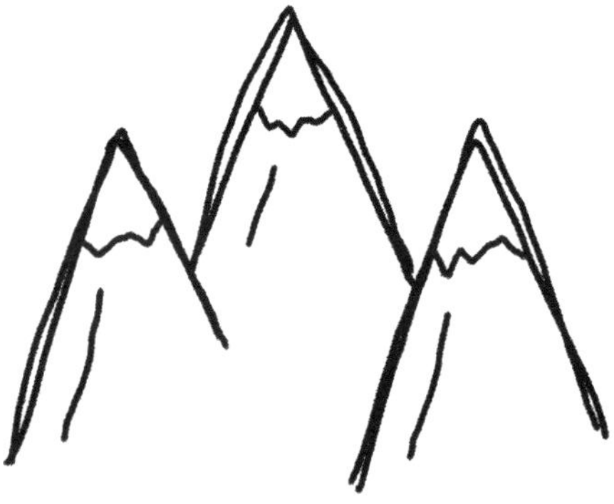

Captain texts

If your Captain could text you throughout the day what would you want them to say?

What would the notification sound like?

doodle starters

Connect the doodles to draw a picture. Add your own doodles too!

If I could have one
SUPERPOWER
it would be...

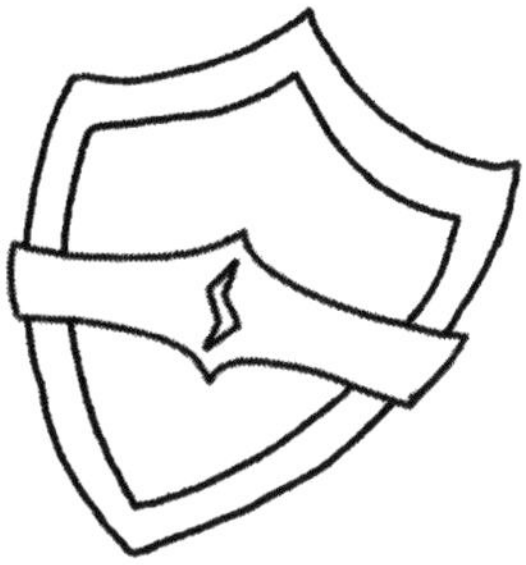

→ Here is what I would do with it:

BE BOLD

What is the most bold thing your captain has ever done?

Captain conversation starters

Name something you were confident about.

What adventures did you have?

What did you get done today?

What problems did you solve?

What did you learn or accomplish today?

What were you not confident about today?

When do you wish your Captain had shown up today?

When did your Captain show up today?

PROCRASTINATION

I keep procrastinating on dealing with my procrastination! Sometimes it helps me because when I run out of time it forces me to do it. Other times it gets me stressed cause everything piles up and I get overwhelmed.

Here is the way I can keep my procrastination in balance.

What I'm procrastinating about	Strategies to keep it under control

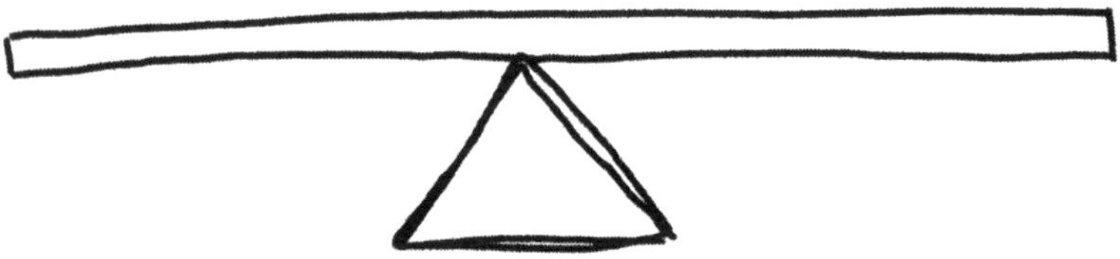

TRYING SOMETHING NEW

Something new you want to try

Pros	Cons

A chance you want to take

Pros	Cons

TAKE A CHANCE

What does your Captain need to know or figure out to feel comfortable doing it?

"You'll never know what you're capable of until you take that first step and just go for it."

– Natasha Hastings

This is what my **CAPTAIN** would do if there were no **LIMITATIONS.**

"Never say never because limits, like fears, are often just an illusion."

– Michael Jordan

Sometimes we just
need to find a way
to get it all out.

scribble this page

(like your life
depended on it!)

scribbling
"~~Painting~~ is just another way of keeping a diary."

– Pablo Picasso

Captain Scavenger Hunt

Find objects that remind you of your Captain, trace or draw them on the page. Or put them in a box for safekeeping!

Something that...

- [ ] is from your favourite game
- [ ] challenges you
- [ ] is your favourite tool
- [ ] makes you feel bold
- [ ] reminds you of a fun time you had
- [ ] is for building things
- [ ] gives me confidence
- [ ] holds things
- [ ] stretches
- [ ] is fun to use outdoors
- [ ] inspires your sense of adventure
- [ ] motivates you
- [ ]

word scramble

Unscramble as many Captain words as you can. Good luck!

decnotnif ______________________________

asvdeoturnu ______________________________

fheullp ______________________________

idveseic ______________________________

obdl ______________________________

edremteind ______________________________

nogzraedi ______________________________

npisdelicdi ______________________________

etaesirsv ______________________________

get out of your comfort zone

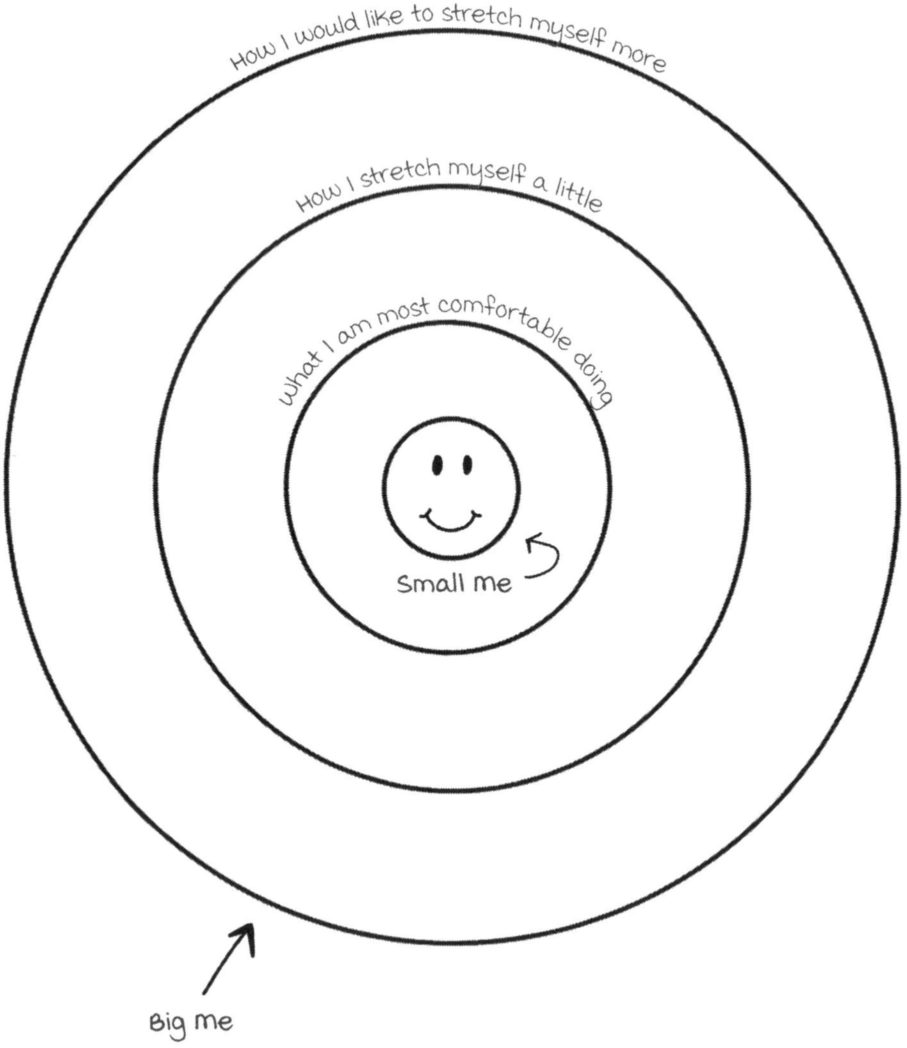

MANDALA

A mandala's pattern helps us focus and colouring them can help process emotions. Colour this amazing mandala design and see how it takes you somewhere new. Hhhhmm. mindfulness.

the colour of my Captain

Close your eyes and imagine a situation where your Captain is feeling great – clear, confident and looking forward to diving in on something.

What colour would you use to describe your Captain right now?

Fill in the circle with that colour.

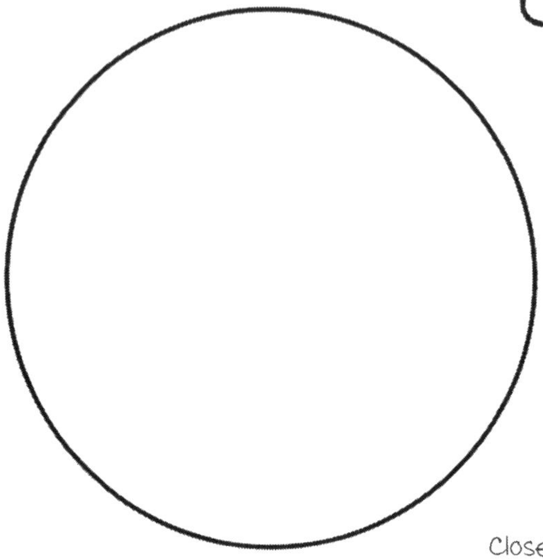

Come back to this page when you are feeling unsure of yourself and need to get back on your game.

Close your eyes and imagine you are breathing in the colour your chose and that it spreads all over your body, especially to the parts that aren't feeling so great.

Exhale slowly.

Repeat this process until you are feeling more like yourself again. Hhhhmm. mindfulness.

Captain yoga poses

Yoga reminds us to listen to our body and pay attention to how we are feeling. Try a few yoga poses and hold them for a little while. Remember to breathe deeply and only do what feels good. Don't forget to switch sides for Half moon, Triangle, Warrior 1 and 2.

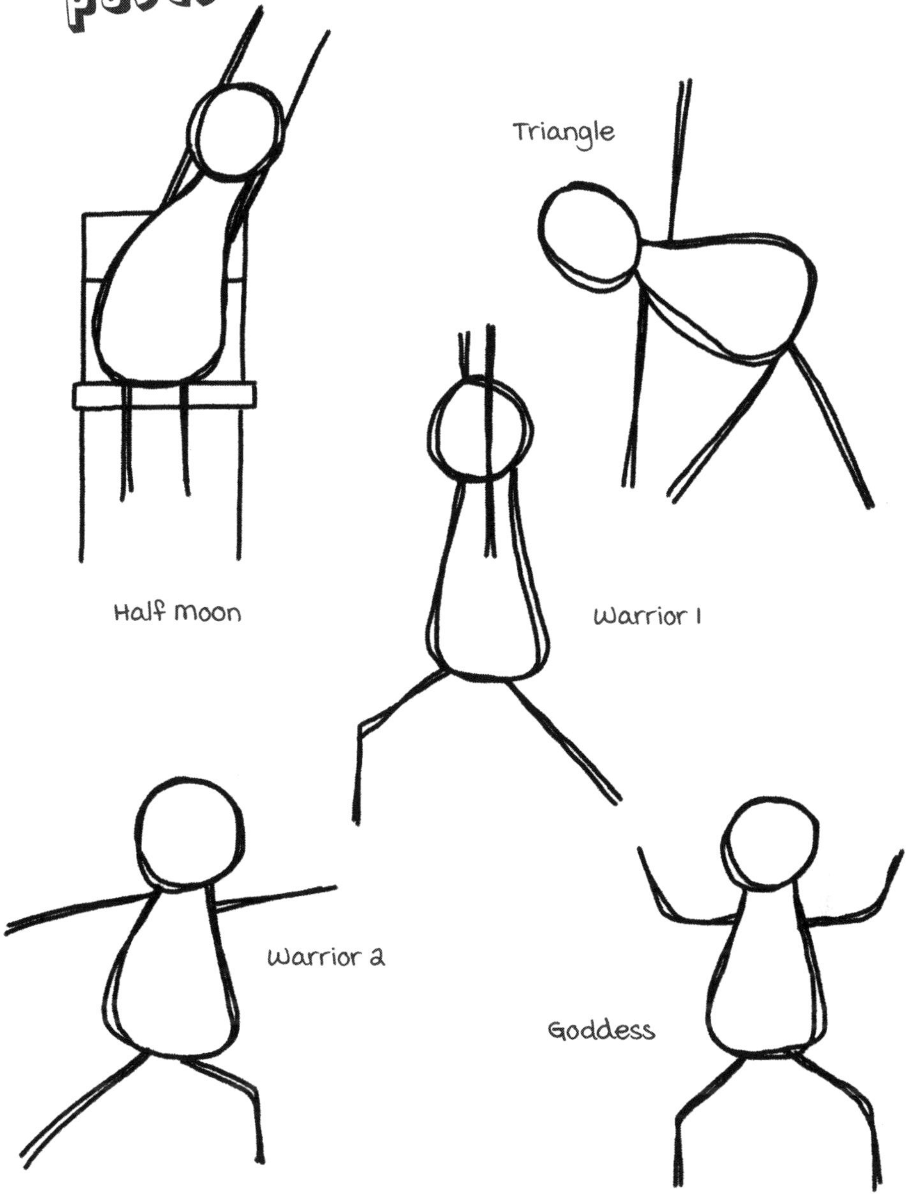

Use these poses whenever you need to get in the Captain zone.

A Captain's plan

Your Poet has a vision and your Captain wants to bring it to life. Go back to page 44 and work backwards from your vision identifying three goals or steps that will get you closer to your vision.

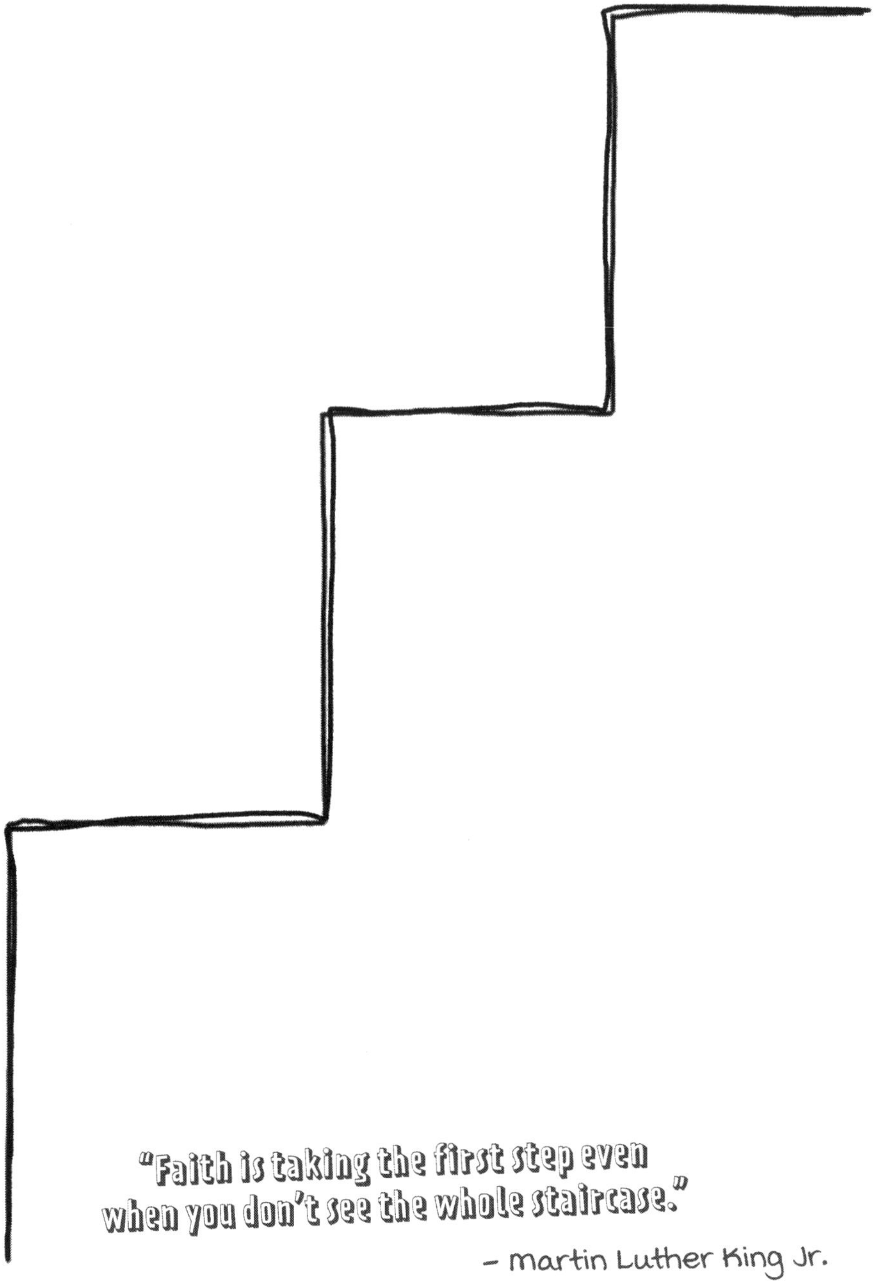

"Faith is taking the first step even when you don't see the whole staircase."

– Martin Luther King Jr.

Captain daily self-assessment

How much of a Captain were you today?

Decisive	1	2	3	4	5
Adventurous	1	2	3	4	5
Helpful	1	2	3	4	5
Bold	1	2	3	4	5
Confident	1	2	3	4	5
Focused	1	2	3	4	5
Determined	1	2	3	4	5
Organized	1	2	3	4	5
Disciplined	1	2	3	4	5
Goal oriented	1	2	3	4	5
Took charge	1	2	3	4	5
Assertive	1	2	3	4	5
Action-Oriented	1	2	3	4	5

an **AFFIRMATION** a day keeps the blues away

Circle the affirmation that is most valuable for you today. Say it three times and repeat it throughout the day! Find an image that represents what it means to you and put it in this page as a bookmark for when you need reminding!

I am ready to stretch beyond my comfort zone.

I don't expect myself to be any more perfect than I would anyone else.

I make important decisions each day.

I am open to trying new things.

Captain Crossword

Watch the video and look for the answers to these questions in this Journal!

Down

1. Sometimes the Captain is ______ and sometimes it is not.
2. My Captain sometimes needs _______ from my Poet to know what to do.
3. The Captain helps us to ____ ourselves.

Across

4. My Captain's confidence comes from ________.
5. My Captain helps me be ____ and share my gifts with the world.
6. My Captain is the part of me that wants to take on _________.
7. My Captain likes to take _____.

ANSWERS: OBVIOUS, GUIDANCE, LEAD, CHALLENGES, CHARGE, BOLD, EXPERIENCE.

CAPTAIN "QUOTES"

"Act as if what you do makes a difference. It does."

– William James

"Life is like riding a bicycle. To keep your balance, you must keep moving."

– Albert Einstein

"We generate fears while we sit. We overcome them by action."

– Dr. Henry Link

"When the whole world is silent, even one voice becomes powerful."

– Malala Yousafzai

"I have not failed. I've just found 10,000 ways that won't work."

– Thomas Edison

"To find yourself, think for yourself."

– Socrates

"What is now proved was once only imagined."

– William Blake

"Integrity is doing the right thing even when no one is watching."

– C.S. Lewis

"We have more possibilities available in each moment than we realize."

– Thich Nhat Hanh

"The bridge between knowledge and skill is practice. The bridge between skill and mastery is time."

– Osu

"I've failed over and over again in my life. And that is why I succeed."

– Michael Jordan

"Be thankful for what you are now, and keep fighting for what you want to be tomorrow."

– Unknown

Better Together

where are you at today?

How do you measure a good day?
What has to happen?

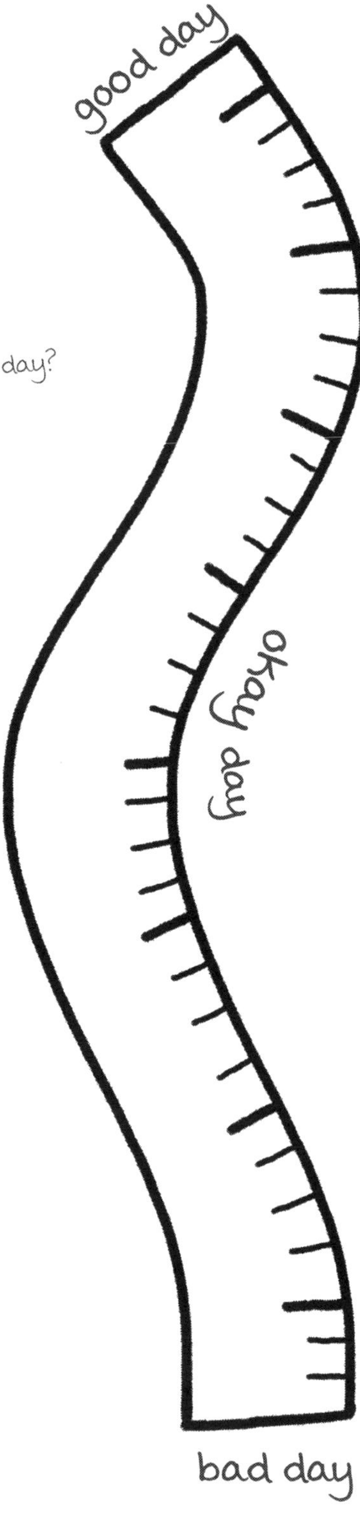

Favourite thing about MYSELF

Some other cool things about me...

"The sky is full of stars and there's room for them all to shine."

– Henry Wadsworth Longfellow

the Captain & Poet are in EVERYONE

Everyone has a Captain and Poet inside them but they show up a little differently for everyone. Which quote from the Captains and Poets in the video did you relate to the most?

- [ ] "If kids are really like more aware of...their Captain and their Poets and what they really do and how they really influence your everyday life without you realizing it, that could really influence the choices that you make in your everyday life."

- [ ] "When my Captain and my Poet work together, it unlocks a happiness in myself. It makes me laugh."

- [ ] "My Captain helps my Poet as a bit of a guide. It helps my Poet really embrace myself and my feelings and it makes my Poet be more vocal with myself and my family."

- [ ] "... my Captain helps my Poet by giving me the power to take action...by actually taking the steps that it needs to make sure that my Poet feels like it's being heard."

- [ ] "My Poet is the one who connects with people to make that friendship stronger and my Captain is the one who's bold enough to go up to someone to make friends with them."

- [ ] "When my Captain and Poet work together, I feel like it makes me the better person. I'm always there for my teammates on the Poet side but I'm also always there to take risks for my teammates."

☐ "my Poet, when I'm in a leadership role, is the kind of the part of me that wants to make connections...So, my, you know Captain, is the part of me that really pushes me to do that."

☐ "With my Captain and my Poet, I have learned that it's okay not to be perfect. ...You don't have to be perfect to be your best self and to be happy."

☐ "—your Poet is the one who gains input on what you want to be, and your Captain is the one who makes small, little decisions to lead up there."

☐ "When you combine your Poet and your Captain you get someone who is doing what they were meant to do, someone who's accomplishing what they are put on this earth to accomplish... making sure that it is my passion...a reflection of who I am as a person and what I feel."

☐ "When the Captain and Poet come together, they give you courage which is different than confidence. Because confidence is thinking you have the ability to do something, but courage is knowing what's right in your heart."

How would you describe how your Captain and Poet work together?

How my **CAPTAIN...**

...helps my **POET.**

How my **POET...**

...helps my **CAPTAIN.**

who are you?

Underline the words that best describe you.
Circle the words that you want to be more of.
Draw a picture of your fabulous self!

AUTHENTIC

COURAGEOUS

PROBLEM SOLVER

RESPONSIBLE

LEADER

COMPASSIONATE

CURIOUS

UNDERSTANDING

RESILIENT

CONSCIENTIOUS

GRATEFUL

THE BEST YOU CAN BE!

ORIGINAL

FUN

How much of a CAPTAIN & Poet have you been lately?

- [ ] Been my true self
- [ ] Solved a problem
- [ ] Been compassionate with myself
- [ ] Been compassionate with others
- [ ] Been grateful for the little things (and the big ones!)
- [ ] Had fun
- [ ] Showed courage
- [ ] Acted on my curiosity about something
- [ ] Bounced back from a setback
- [ ] Showed up as a leader when it was needed

→ Give yourself a point for each answer. Add them up and check your score!

Captain and Poet on the bench 0–3 Points

The world is waiting for you! Spend some time with people you are most comfortable with and explore.

Captain and Poet emerging 4–6 Points

Watch out world. You are about to bust out of your cocoon into a beautiful butterfly. Pick something from the list above and give it a try!

Captain and Poet champion 7–8 Points

You are already recognized as being one of the most authentic and fabulous people out there. Keep your Captain and Poet close as you climb the next mountain!

Captain & Poet wizard! 9–10 Points

You are totally in the zone and you have discovered the magical combination of you! Don't get discouraged if you get off track. That just means there is more for you to discover!

the meaning behind my NAME

Research or ask your family about your name. What does it mean? What is it's history? Where does it come from?

The Captain and Poet both show up in the meaning of my name because...

crazy Captain & Poet COMBINATIONS

Pick one characteristic from the Poet and one from the Captain. What are we like when we combine them? What becomes possible that wasn't possible before?

Poet

- Creative
- Artistic
- Empathic
- Imaginative
- Reflective
- Perceptive
- Listens well
- Caring
- Kind
- Observant
- Sensitive
- Intuitive
- Understanding

Captain

- Decisive
- Adventurous
- Helpful
- Bold
- Confident
- Focused
- Determined
- Organized
- Disciplined
- Goal oriented
- Takes charge
- Assertive
- Action-Oriented

Examples

Adventurous + Imaginative
= making up crazy, fun games with your friends.

Bold + Empathetic
= Stopping bullies in their tracks.

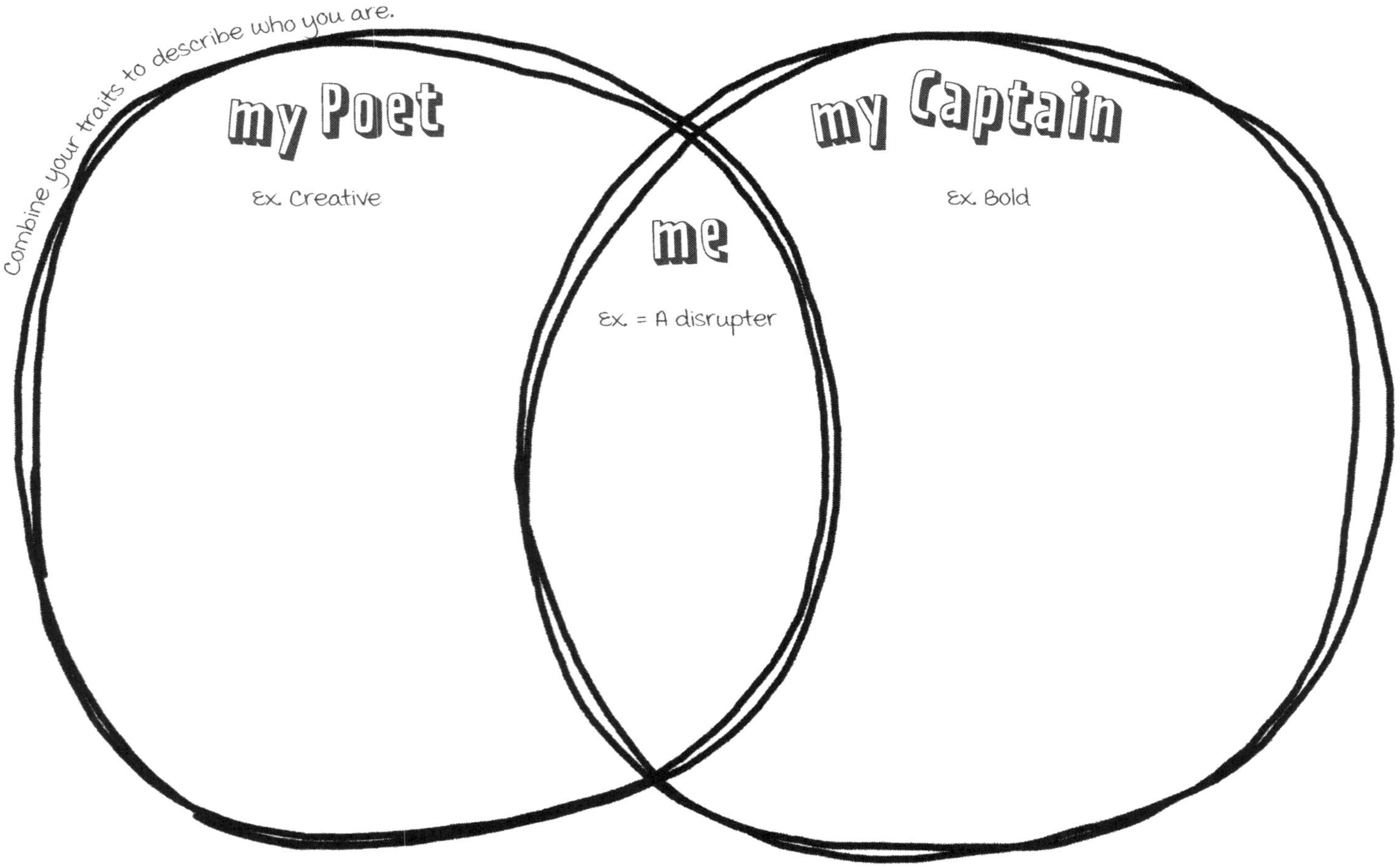
Combine your traits to describe who you are.
my Poet
Ex. Creative
me
Ex. = A disrupter
my Captain
Ex. Bold

my favourite things

memory

junk food

place

song

celebrity

musician

movie

book

comeback

A day in my LIFE

Describe what your Captain and Poet like to do throughout the day.

RITUALS

Rituals help us bring meaning and purpose to our life. They also help us to even out the ups and downs of life by reminding us of what is important.

Create a morning ritual to kick off each day in a positive way. It could be a meditation, an exercise routine, setting an intention for the day, or repeating a mantra or affirmation before you get out of bed. Draw a picture of it and how it will make you feel here.

Create an evening ritual to close off each day in a positive way. It could be a meditation, asking yourself how you did on your intention, accepting something that happened and letting it go, or repeating a mantra or affirmation before you go to sleep. Draw a picture of it and how it will make you feel here.

FIRSTS

Our first time trying something can be an important memory for us. It can also help us learn what is important to us so we can make good choices in the future. Make a list of firsts in your life and and note what you want more of and what you are okay to leave behind about that experience.

	What you want more of	What you want to leave behind
First Friend		
First Love		
First Pet		
First Team		
First Holiday		
First Adventure		
First thing I bought		
First Performance		
First Teacher		
First Collection		
First time I stood up for myself		
First ____________		

my Captain & Poet playlist

Songs that inspire the Captain and Poet in me.

write a review for the **BEST** or **WORST** concert you have been to

Rate it!

write a review

Write a review of a movie, album, TV show, brand of clothing or even a recent celebrity blunder. What did your Captain and Poet like and dislike about it? Give it a catchy headline and give everyone the full scoop.

Rate it!

Advice for my YOUNGER self.

Think back to a time you were struggling.
What advice would you give yourself now?

"Everything will be okay in the end.
If it's not okay it's not the end."

- John Lennon

"There is no passion to be found playing small—in settling for a life that is less than the one you are capable of living."

– Nelson Mandela

What do you know now that you want to remember when you are older? Give your future self some advice to hold onto.

Advice for my OLDER self.

Imagining who we want to be helps us create the life we want. Write a letter to yourself in 5–10 years that acknowledges what an amazing person you have become!

A letter to my FUTURE self.

A letter to my PAST self.

Think of something that happened that still preoccupies your mind sometimes. Write yourself a letter that shows compassion and understanding for what you went through.

birthday reflections

Birthdays are a time to celebrate who you are.

The thing I loved about being age _______ is...

What I am looking forward to about being age ________ is...

Give yourself a gift! Something I wish for myself this year is...

a PICTURE is worth 1000 words

Create a symbol or icon that reminds you of the following things.

What makes you special

What is inside of you

What happiness feels like

How others see you

What is important to you

What family means to you

What friendship means to you.

Better Together maze

Being your best self is a never-ending journey of self-discovery.

How many **WORDS** can you make from...

Captain & Poet?

would you rather?

Be a director	or	Be an actor
Have a guardian angel	or	Be a guardian angel
Sleep in a marshmallow bed	or	Eat a marshmallow the size of a bed
Clean your room everyday	or	Clean your sibling's room once a month
Score on the wrong goal	or	Miss the winning pass
Be a couch potato	or	Eat a potato you found in the couch
Know everything there is to know	or	Discover the world around you for the first time each day
Listen to your favourite song 100 times in a row and get sick of it	or	Never hear that song again but remember it fondly
Constant change	or	Nothing ever changes
Attend only concerts	or	Attend only sporting events
Own a time machine	or	Own a teleporter

a side of me **EVERYONE** knows

something you wish everyone knew.

a side of me **VERY FEW** people know

two truths and a lie

write down two things that are true about you and one lie. See if others can guess which is the lie.

1.

2.

3.

Interview someone about **YOU!**

/5

→ make up 5 questions about yourself. Give them a score to see how well they know you.

- [ ]
- [ ]
- [ ]
- [ ]
- [ ]

something I learned about

MYSELF recently

the constellation of you

Did you know that the stars in the sky are constantly moving? Just like us, they are changing and shifting each day. Just like constellations, each of us is a unique combination. Your Captain and Poet are there to help guide you to shine as brightly as you are meant to.

Design your own unique constellation to remind you that you have a special place in a vast universe and that you make a difference just by shining who you are.

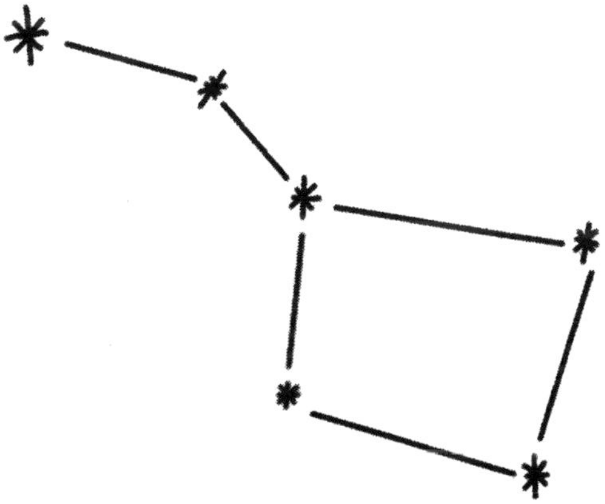

making our own meaning

Get your Poet's creative juices working and finish the following popular phrases in your own way.

If you don't know the originals look up "popular idioms" and see if you can find it!

Life is like...

Better late than...

Good things come to those who...

The best things in life...

Time flies when you...

Research where they each came from!

self - care checklist

We all need outlets when we are feeling stressed or down. Which of these are your go-to's? Add two more to the list that you can practice.

- [ ] Shoot hoops
- [ ] Bake
- [ ] Play a game
- [ ] Call or text a friend
- [ ] Cuddle with your pet
- [ ] Take a walk
- [ ] Paint or draw something
- [ ] Listen to music
- [ ] Breathe
- [ ] Try a new look
- [ ]
- [ ]

add a couple more!

when i am sad i...

- [ ] Spend time in my room
- [ ] Share how I am feeling with someone
- [ ] Get quiet or moody
- [ ] Watch a movie
- [ ]

← Fill in your own!

How can your Captain and Poet help you deal better with your sadness?

when i am mad i...

- [ ] express it loudly and clearly
- [ ] Walk away
- [ ] Get really quiet
- [ ] Dwell on it
- [ ]

← Fill in your own!

How can your Captain and Poet help you deal better with your anger?

THE SHAPE OF A CAPTAIN & POET

Write the words
Captain and Poet in
different ways with lots
of different Captain
and Poet fonts.

mindfulness exercise

Lie down and starting at your toes, slowly scan your body all the way up for two or more minutes as you breathe slowly.

Notice areas of tension. Just pause and observe them for a few seconds. Then keep going.

If the feelingin your body had a colour, what colour would it be?

Colour it here

Now imagine that colour getting thinner and thinner and eventually disappearing.

What did you notice just happened to you when you did that? Hhhhmm. mindfulness...

dream journal

Writing down your dreams helps you remember them. Share a recent dream. How did your Captain and Poet show up to help you? Where were they struggling? What message does your dream have for you?

word scramble

Unscramble as many Captain and Poet words as you can. Good luck!

guatefrl ______________________________

eouragcous ______________________________

raelde ______________________________

nathiceut ______________________________

soriuuc ______________________________

inuqnue ______________________________

nompatsiosace ______________________________

linrestie ______________________________

piecing together who you are

Being the Captain and Poet you were meant to be takes practice.
Colour a puzzle piece for the Captain and the Poet each time you act like one.

create an **EMOJI** of your Captain & Poet

How could you use it while texting?

Captain & Poet Horoscopes

Aries
(mar 21 – Apr 20)

Your Poet is passionate and processes things quickly. Your Captain is bold, independent, confident and adventurous. Your Captain's enthusiasm for life helps you share yourself with others and open up new possibilities to explore. Together they help you balance giving and receiving, be a good team player and lead fearlessly. Watch out world!

Taurus
(Apr 21 – may 21)

Your Captain is pragmatic, persevering and dependable. Your Poet is gentle and devoted and appreciates the beauty in the world. Together they help you know where you stand on things. But your Captain can be stubborn so your Poet can help you bend and be open to change. Change can be good. Balancing your Captain and Poet is the key.

Gemini
(may 22 – June 21)

Your Poet is a thoughtful, gifted communicator and your Captain balances your emotions with your intellect making you gifted at connecting with others. Your Poet's inquisitive nature and your Captain's craving for experience make life an adventure. You love problem solving and definitely don't like getting stuck in a routine. But most of all you want to make a difference!

Cancer
(June 22 – July 22)

Your nurturing, empathetic and sentimental Poet feels it all and their intuition is strong. Your protective and loyal Captain helps you navigate situations in the best interests of you and those around you. Even though your Poet can be moody, they always help you sense which direction to go. Your best decisions are those where the Captain consults the Poet and is fueled by putting your heart into things.

Leo
(July 23 – Aug 22)

Your confident Captain opens doors and does not shy away from the spotlight. Your warm-hearted Poet is humourous, joyful and creative. Your Poet helps you to be self-aware and to consider the needs of others while the Captain satisfies your need for growth. Together they help you to achieve your dreams and enjoy all life has to offer while caring for those close to you along the way.

Virgo
(Aug 23 – Sept 22)

Your serious and detail-oriented Poet is sometimes a little shy about expressing themselves. Your hardworking Captain is organized, sensible and loves to improve things but can sometimes be a perfectionist. When you keep them in balance, they help you bring your dreams to life. Don't forget to let your kind Poet give you a hug once in a while along the way!

Libra
(Sept 23 - Oct 22)

Your sensitive and romantic Poet is a brilliant communicator. Your proud and intellectual Captain values fairness and balance. Together, they help you be diplomatic in all your relationships. You sometimes like to avoid conflict but together your Captain and Poet make you a brilliant negotiator. Your Captain's best decisions are when you consult what your inner Poet needs and check your gut.

Scorpio
(Oct 23 - Nov 21)

Your intense and passionate Poet partners with your assertive and resourceful Captain to get what you want. Together, they make you a highly focused person in every aspect of your life. You are an all-or-nothing kind of person which makes you a great friend and also fearless in facing challenges. Your Captain likes to research things to satisfy your Poet's desire for truth. You love the journey and to guide others along the way.

Sagittarius
(Nov 22 - Dec 21)

Your Captain is a positive, enthusiastic and loves to be spontaneous. Your Poet connects with everyone because they love to talk about anything and everything and can help your Captain to be more diplomatic. Together, they seek new experiences, ideas and relationships that help you learn about yourself and the world around you. Your Captain seeks freedom while your Poet seeks truth. What a magical combination!

Capricorn
(Dec 22 - Jan 20)

Your Captain is patient, responsible, practical, hard-working and never gives up. While reserved emotionally, you invest in long-term relationships and use your Poet's humour to connect with others. Your Poet can help you take different perspectives when needed. Together, your Captain and Poet help you learn from experience and go after your dreams with a mature attitude.

Aquarius
(Jan 21 - Feb 19)

Your idealistic and contemplative Poet cares deeply about humanity and the future. Your independent Captain is good at seeing the big picture and loves to fight for freedom. Your Poet helps your Captain keep an open heart and mind and not be so stubborn :) Together, they help you think outside the box, live from your own beliefs and follow the beat of your own drum.

Pisces
(Feb 20 - Mar 20)

You have a heavy dose of Poet as an imaginative dreamer, a sensitive empath, an intuitive and a deep feeler. Your Captain is highly adaptive, friendly and helpful but needs to keep boundaries with others and remind you to stay grounded when you start spending too much time in the clouds. Together, they help you to constantly recreate yourself.

off the rack →

What you wear is an expression of who you are. Dress up like your Poet is feeling all the feels and your Captain is ready to bend the rules. Shorts in winter? An outrageous hat? Plaid AND polka-dot?

my room is my oyster

You probably spend a lot of time in your room. Describe or draw it. Show how the Captain and Poet show up in the way you decorate your room.

P.S. Clean up! Ask your Captain for help getting started :)

BELONGING - O - METER

To Belong or not to belong? That is the question.

	The areas of my life where I don't feel like I belong	The areas of my life where I don't fit in well	The areas of my life where I fit in okay	The areas of my life where I fit in easily	The areas of my life where I feel like I belong
How my Captain can help me move a step to the right.					
How my Poet can help me move a step to the right.					

"Belonging is being accepted for you. Fitting in is being accepted for being like everyone else."

– Brené Brown

Captain & Poet friend checklist

A good friend will...

- [ ] Tell me the truth
- [ ] See the best in me
- [ ] Respect my wishes
- [ ] Listen without looking at their phone
- [ ] Not talk about me behind my back
- [ ] Keep my secrets
- [ ] Encourage me to do what is best for me
- [ ] Understand when I need space
- [ ] Apologize when they make a mistake
- [ ] make me laugh
- [ ] Read my body language
- [ ] make me feel comfortable being myself
- [ ] Give me a pat on the shoulder or a hug when I am having a bad day
- [ ]

Captain & Poet besties

Describe your ideal friend.
How do their Captain and Poet help them be a great friend?

How do your Captain and Poet help you be a great friend?

friendship rainbow

The way you think and feel is influenced by the people around you. Who is in your rainbow? Are they making your rainbow brighter or dimmer? Fill in the names of the seven people you spend the most time with. Draw in each colour of the rainbow to show how much spending time with that person brightens your life.

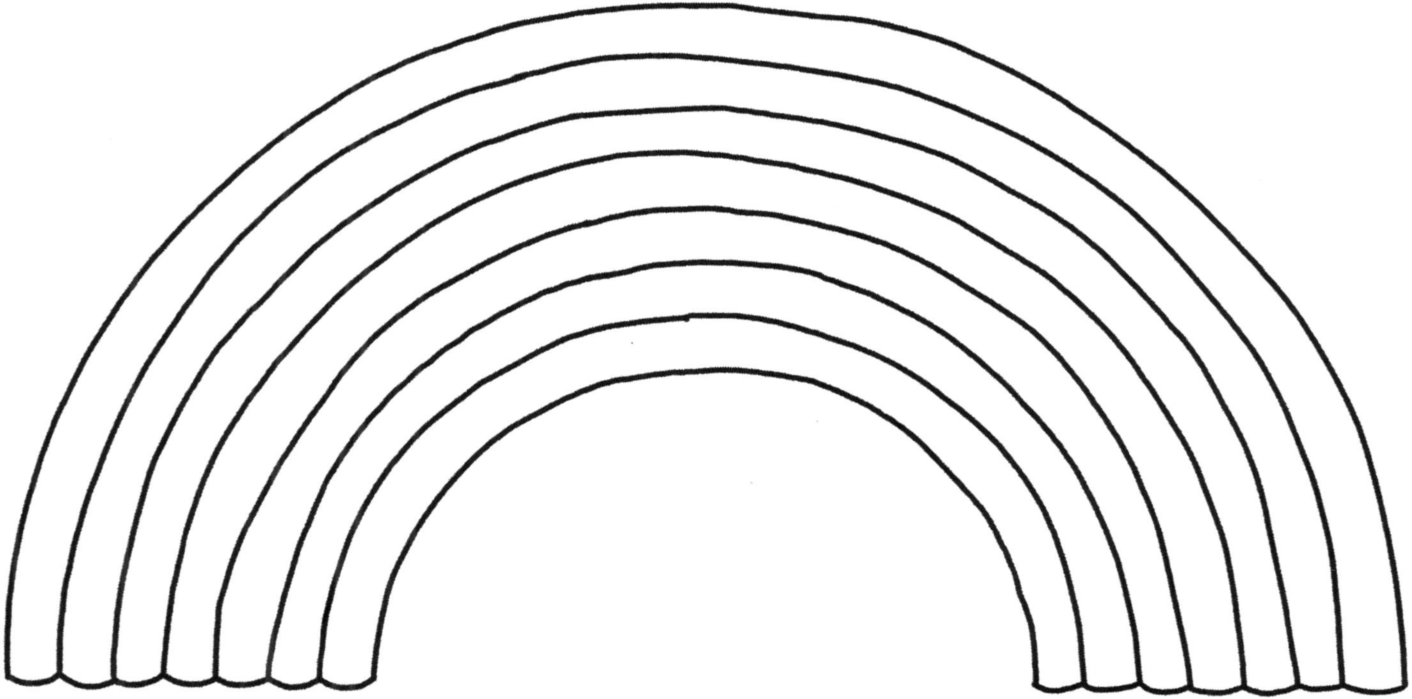

friend profiles

Pick three friends and describe their Captains and their Poets. Why do you appreciate each of them?

a picture of them

your friends know you best

What would your friends say about you?
Text your bestie and see what they think!

What they like the most about you...

How they see your Poet...

How they see your Captain...

When you are at your best you...

What they want for you...

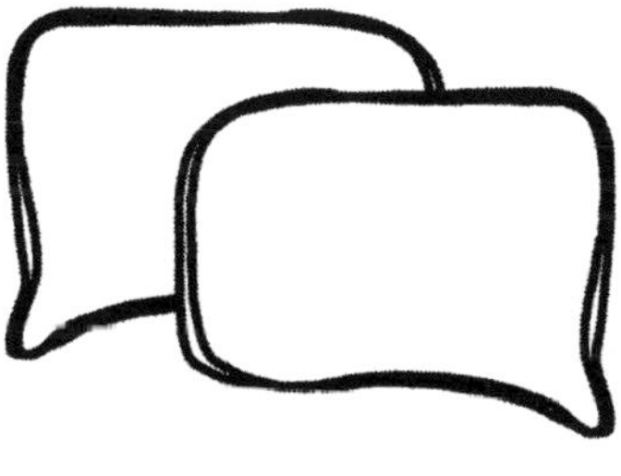

the cure for drama

Life can be full of drama sometimes. Think of a recent situation where there was a lot of drama. How can your Poet remind you of what is important in that situation? How can your Captain help you manage it calmly?

design your own friendship bracelet

make a bracelet for a friend with the inside engraved with their Captain and Poet traits and the outside with something that reminds you of them.

"The only way to have a [Captain and Poet] friend is to be a [Captain and Poet] friend."

– Ralph Waldo Emerson

Captain & Poet teammates

make a list of the Captain and Poet traits that you see on your team. Circle the ones that you value the most.

Teammate	Captain Trait	Poet Trait

Why is it important to have teammates with different traits?

ultimate Captains & Poets team

Create the ultimate sports team with athletes who embody the Captain and Poet. Label their jerseys with their best traits. If they are from different sports make up a new game for them to play!

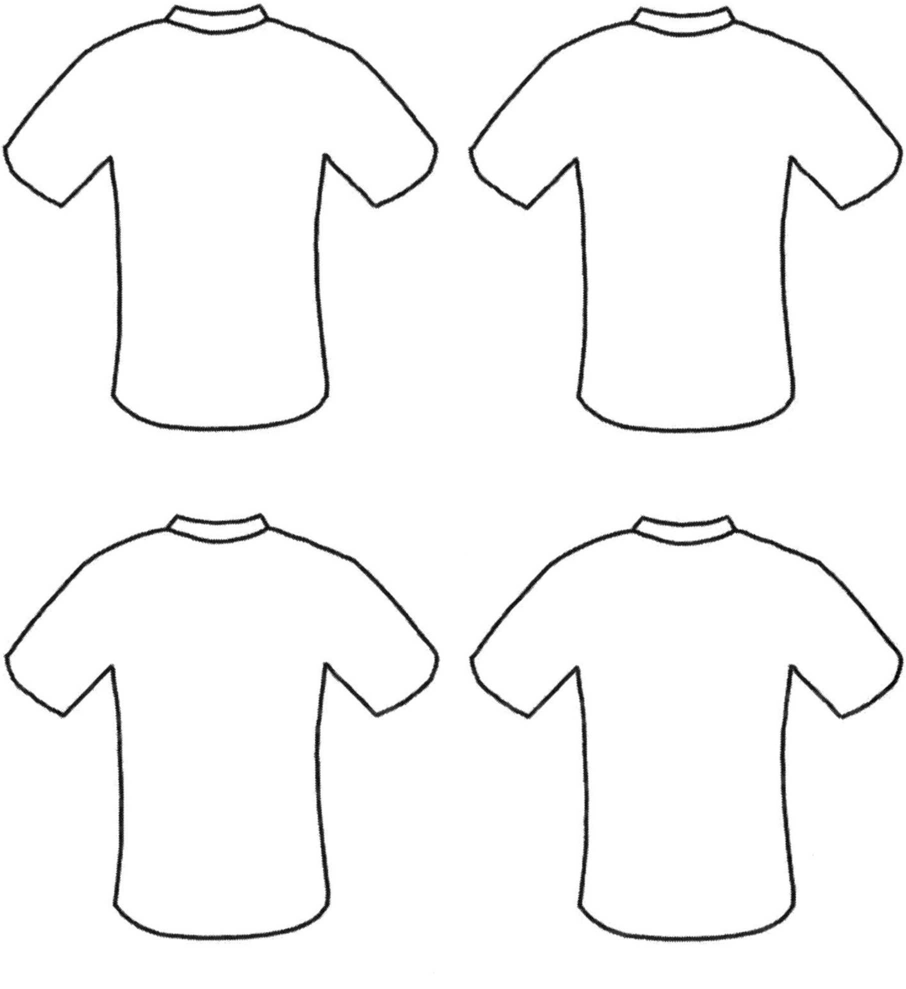

"The strength of the team is each individual player. The strength of each member is the team."

– Phil Jackson

How SOCIAL are your Captain & Poet?

1. When it comes to friends:

A) I like to keep it to one bestie.

B) A few close friends is best.

C) A variety of buddies keeps it interesting.

D) The more the merrier.

2. A good friend is someone who:

A) Is there when I really need them.

B) Keeps in touch and doesn't get hung up if we don't talk every day.

C) I can pick back up with them after a few months and it's like nothing has changed.

D) Keeps me in the loop on what's up.

3. Your friend is upset about something so you:

A) Give them a knowing glance and tell them everything will be okay.

B) Tell them to reach out when they are ready to talk about it.

C) Hang out with them until they are ready to talk.

D) Invite them to a hangout with some other friends to get their mind off things.

4. You're hanging with friends and the conversation dies down so you:

A) Feel a bit awkward and wait for someone else to break the silence.

B) Enjoy the silence. It will pass.

C) See it as an opportunity to tell that new joke you just heard.

D) Check your phone to see if there is anything interesting going on.

5. It's a new school year and it's the first time seeing a friend since last year. You make eye contact with them in the hallway while they are talking to someone else. You:

A) Let them make the first move.

B) Smile as you walk by.

C) Say "Hi" and suggest you meet up at lunch.

D) Walk over and introduce yourself to the person they are talking to.

6. When it comes to popularity contests:

A) You are happy to keep to people from your classes, teams and clubs.

B) You go to the beat of your own drum. Who wants to be a flash in the pan?

C) You make an effort to be friends with people you are drawn to, regardless of who they hangout with.

D) Your friend group is always evolving and expanding. You may not be the most popular but everybody knows you.

→ Check Your Score! Count up the number of answers for each category:

Mostly A's

Your Captain and Poet are a bit reserved but they have figured out how to navigate the world.

Mostly B's

Your Captain and Poet are independent but value good relationships with other Captains and Poets.

Mostly C's

Your Captain and Poet enjoy connecting with others' Captains and Poets when life offers up the opportunity.

Mostly D's

Your Captain and Poet seek a busy social life. So many friends, so little time.

Send a POSTCARD

Choose a photo that shows what your life is like at its best.
Write a special note on the back and send it to someone!

awesome, authentic, amazing adjectives

Pick five words from the list that describe five people in your life that you admire. Write their name under the word.

Adventurous

Reflective

Creative

Focused

Helpful

Perceptive

Artistic

Persistent

Bold

Listens

Empathetic

Experienced

Confident

Observant

Imaginative

Organized

Decisive

Wise

A Captain & Poet's best friend

Have you ever wondered what your pet is trying to say to you when they stare at you?

How are you a Captain with them?
How are you a Poet with them?

family profile

Pick someone from your family and describe their Captain and Poet in detail.

a picture of them

Interview an older FAMILY MEMBER or FRIEND

1. What is your first memory?

2. What was the most important day of your life?

3. What was the happiest day of your life?

4. What was the best decision you ever made?

5. How have your Captain and Poet helped you along the way?

6. What would you change about your life?

7. What would you like to be remembered for?

Captain & Poet role models

Describe your favourite teacher, coach or counsellor. How do their Captain and Poet make them such a great person?

a picture of them

the most **important** person in my **life**

Reflect on someone that means the world to you. What is it you love about their Captain and Poet?

thank you for **INSPIRING** me

Write a letter to someone that has inspired you. It could be a coach, a teacher, a friend, etc. Tell them how they inspired you. Your Poet can help you speak from the heart. Your Captain can help you be bold enough to give it to them.

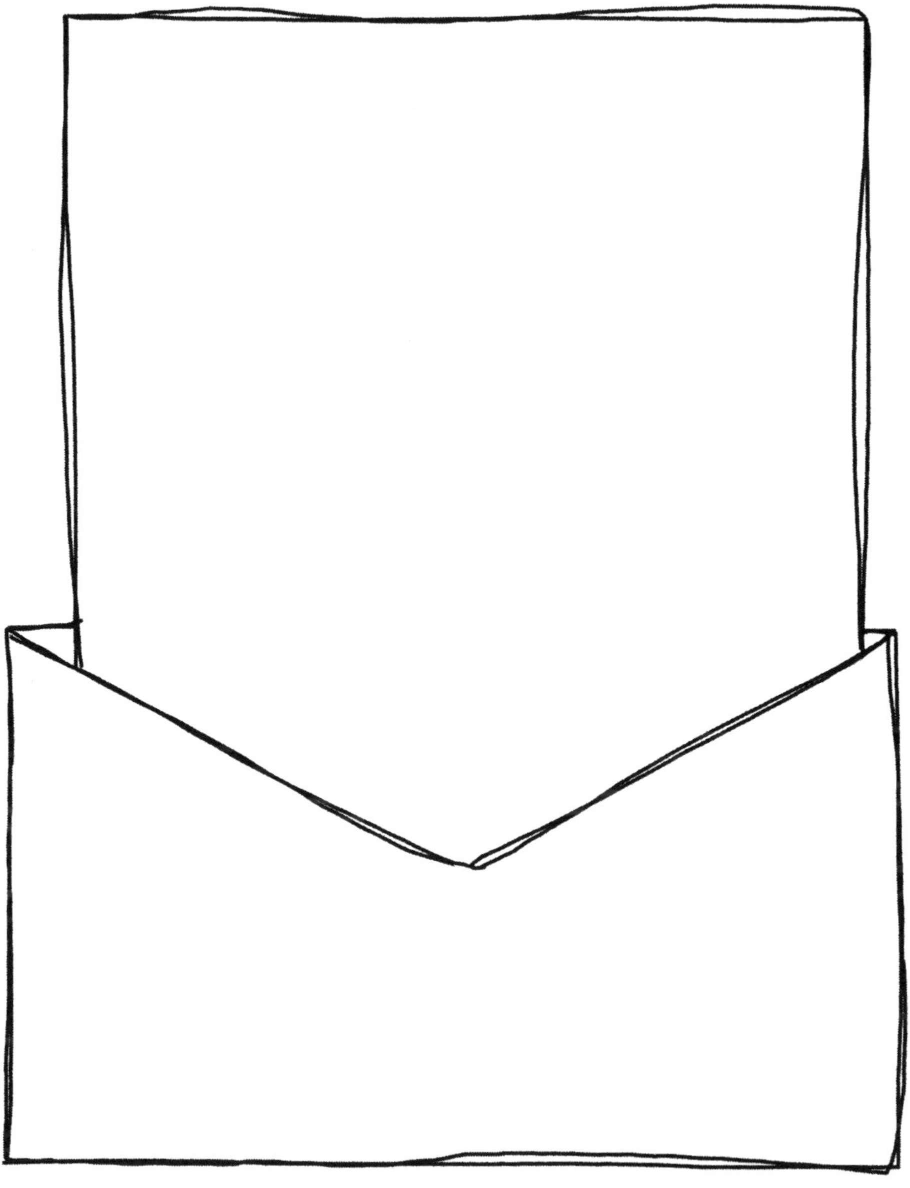

Captain & poet conversation starters

Did any problems or challenges come up today? How did your Captain and Poet help solve them?

Did you have any moments where you didn't feel like you were being yourself today? What happened?

How were you your best self today?

Did your Poet come up with any great ideas? How did your Captain help you try them out?

What made you happy today?

What was the funniest thing that happened today?

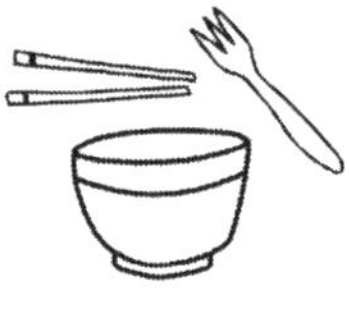

How did you help someone today?

Did you feel what someone else was feeling? What did you do about it?

change barometer

→ How much change is happening in your life right now?

- [ ] my whole world is in flux 

- [ ] Some stuff changing for sure. 

- [ ] like Nothing! 

↪ How can your Captain and Poet help you deal with it?

What were the highs and the lows over the past few months?

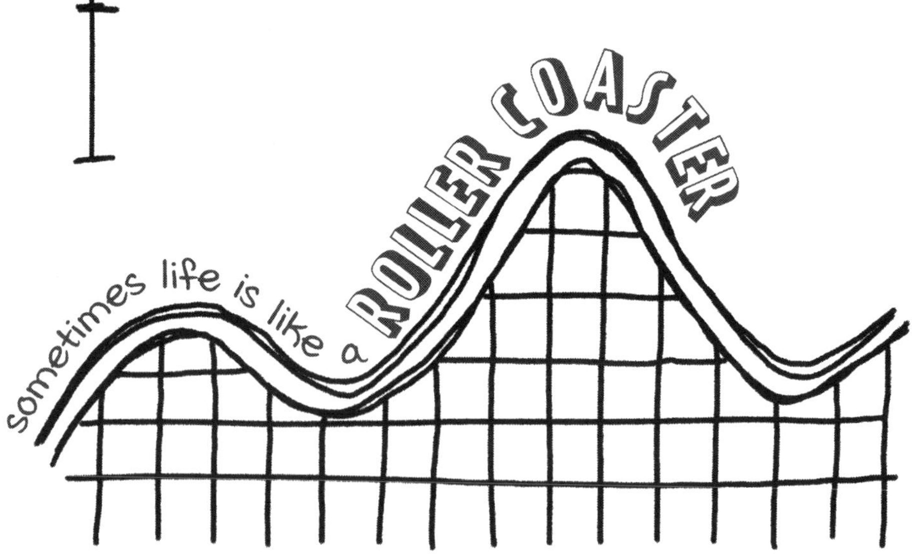

What began and ended during that time?

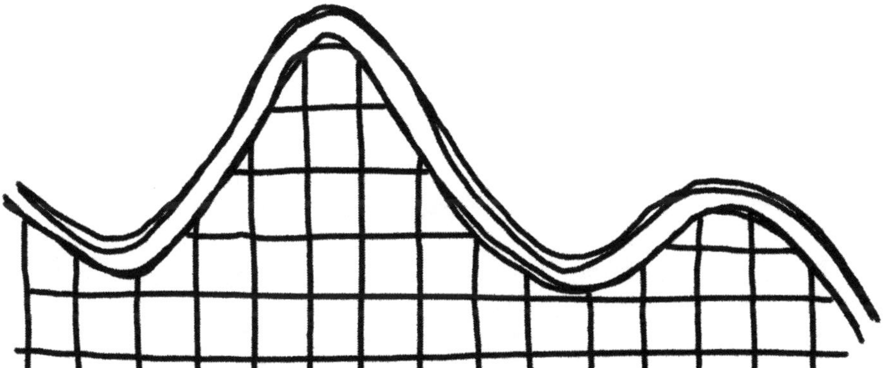

STRESSED OUT!

What are the top three things stressing you out in your life right now?

1.

2.

3.

How can your Captain and Poet help?

things I can CONTROL

things I can't CONTROL

What to do about it?
Help me Captain!

How to shift my
perspective. Help me Poet!

"When we are no longer able to change a situation, we are challenged to change ourselves."

– Viktor E. Frankl

solving problems

"A problem is a chance for you to do your best."

– Duke Ellington

1. Sometimes problems are easy to solve and sometimes they are hard. I sometimes get stuck when I have a problem because...

2. A problem I have to solve right now is...

3. My Poet can help me to solve this problem by reminding me of what is important to me. What is important to me in this situation is...

4. My Poet can also help me use my imagination to come up with ideas like...

5. My Captain can help me to solve this problem by reminding me I have solved problems before. A similar problem I solved before was...

6. My Captain can also encourage me to take a step or make a plan. This can help me with this problem I am having right now by...

ambiguous situations

The Captain and Poet help make things clearer for us. What would you do in these situations?

You win a million dollars.

A friend forgets their lunch.

You get in trouble for something you didnt do.

You suspect someone is getting bullied across the schoolyard.

Someone you don't know has a "kick me" sign on the back of their shirt.

You forget the lyrics to a song you are performing (but no one knows the song).

Someone posted a really unflattering picture of you on social media.

practice making mistakes

We feel so much pressure to be perfect sometimes. It's a good idea to remind ourselves that being perfect isn't possible.

Try writing your name with your opposite hand below. What did you do well? Give yourself some credit and maybe even have a good laugh! Now try it five more times. Not only did you just get better at something difficult, you just rewired your brain and probably your attitude too!

"Anyone who has never made a mistake has never tried anything new."

– Albert Einstein

You just learned how to learn something new. Now try something new that you know is going to take some practice and see what happens.

trouble

Getting in trouble often leaves us feeling terrible, confused and distressed.
When was the last time you got in trouble?

How can your Captain and Poet help you understand that experience better?

stop! start. continue...

Try this exercise whenever you are trying to figure out how to make a situation, a relationship or an approach better.

Situation	Stop
Ex. my friend circle is not working so well	Ex. Trying so hard
Start	**Continue**
Ex. Spending time with new people	Ex. Being open and friendly with everyone

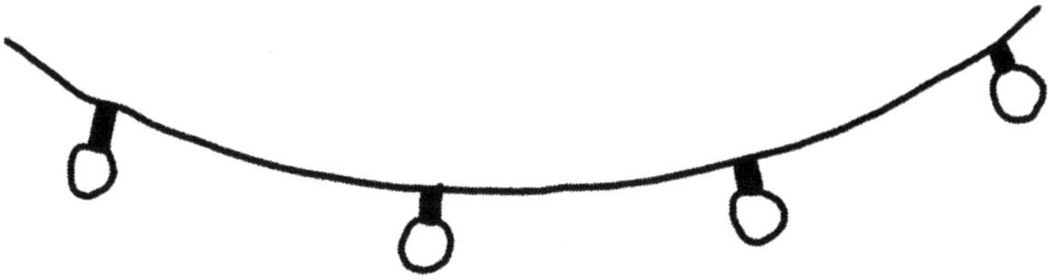

Captain & Poet moments

Happiness comes to us as moments in time. String together a few of your happy moments lalely.

stuck in my head

Things you can't stop thinking about.

Tip: If it's a song that is stuck in your head, try singing a song from an opposite genre. Watch out Hip Hop. Here come's some Opera!

stuck in my heart

Something that is so important to you you can't let go of it.

No tips here.
When something is in your heart it often stays there forever...

Tip: Learning something new is a good way to get your brain unstuck. Try looking up the term "earworm". If you don't it might get stuck in your head too!

mindfulness exercise

Notice your breathing. Is it shallow?
Are you using your chest or your belly as well?

Try using both and breathe in for 5 seconds,
hold for 5 seconds, breathe out for 5 seconds.
Repeat 5 times.

What did you notice just happened
to you when you did that?
Hhhhmm. mindfulness...

What do you have the URGE to do right this second?

What does your Poet say?
What does your Captain say?

What is holding you back?

How would this help you be your authentic self?

What are you ready for next?

we are what we THINK

Think of something that made you angry recently. You probably feel angry now, right?

Think of something that made you happy recently. You probably feel happy now, right?

It is important to pay attention to how much time you are spending thinking about certain things. make a list of a few things that have been on your mind lately. Now, use the pie below to decide how big of a slice you want to give to each of them. Draw the pieces in different sizes below.

make sure you leave a big piece for happy thoughts!

Pick up litter off the sidewalk

Volunteer to do something

good deeds I can do this week

Your Captain and Poet want to make a difference!

Smile at a stranger

Compliment someone

Pitch in and do some chores around the house

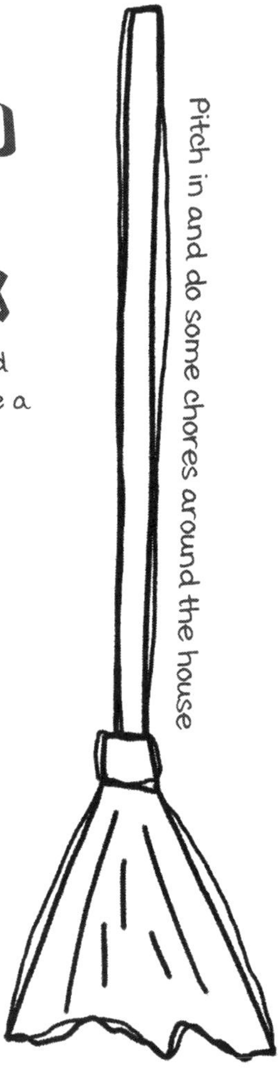

compliments

Compliments remind us how the world sees us. Come up with three compliments you can give today that help others see the best in themselves.. Include one for yourself as well!

finish the spiral story

There once was a Captain who met a Poet...

daydreaming

If you could skip school and do anything today what would you do?

There's no harm in daydreaming! It's your Poet telling you what you need more of in your life.

202_ year in review

Reflect on the year that just passed to help you create an even better year this year.

A lesson I learned

Something I lost

Something I gained

How I explored myself more

How I shared myself more

Something I am proud of

What I would change if I had the chance

What I want to leave behind

What I want to carry forward next year

A word that describes the year

A word that I want to focus on for the year ahead

week in review

High point of the week

Low point of the week

Accomplishments

How I celebrated

Time wasters

Intention for next week!

reality check

What didn't totally suck today?

What was actually kind of cool today?

What might be good about tomorrow?

daily self - assessment

How much of a Captain and Poet were you today?

Authentic	1	2	3	4	5
Compassionate	1	2	3	4	5
Courageous	1	2	3	4	5
Problem solver	1	2	3	4	5
Curious	1	2	3	4	5
Resilient	1	2	3	4	5
Grateful	1	2	3	4	5
Fun	1	2	3	4	5
Leader	1	2	3	4	5

a word is worth a ~~THOUSAND~~ PICTURES

at least a couple of

write the words you felt today in the size that you felt them. For example, if your day was mostly happy make the word HAPPY really big and in the middle of the page. use your own words as well!

Happiness	Frustration	Worry	Love
Fear	Boredom	Guilt	Anger
Pain	Stress	Relief	Kindness
Sadness	Hope	Anxiety	Connection

showing up

How well did I show up today?

/10

How did I show up well?

How do I need to show up more?

The biggest **CHALLENGE** I faced today was...

If you could have done one thing **DIFFERENTLY** today, what would it have been?

Where could your Captain and Poet have shown up more to help you?

Remember a GOOD day!

What happened?

Why was it such a great day?

Which part do you want to repeat again and again and again?

How can you have more great days like this?

Look back at this when you need it!

Imagine your BEST day ever!

Even as we get older our Captain and Poet still like to play! Imagine your perfect day where your Captain and Poet are both having fun!

Now take one step toward making that happen.

"Live out of your imagination, not your history."

– Stephen Covey

What do you spend too much time doing?

What do you spend too little time doing?

Spending your time

Time is like money – we want to spend it wisely to be the happiest we can be.

Habit tracker

We are all creatures of habit and our habits make up our days and our days make up our life. List the habits you want to have to create a better life and draw a symbol or picture to show why this is important.

Give yourself a check mark each time you do it. Give yourself a star if it was a great effort! Ask your Captain and Poet to help you keep up the great work!

Example:										

goal setting

Write down a goal you want to accomplish:

Check in regularly to give an update on how you are doing.

Date	Check-in

3 things I want to accomplish before I **GRADUATE**

→ **1.**

→ **2.**

→ **3.**

"You already have everything you need inside of you right now, today."

– Alicia Keys

something you regret

Regret is a strong feeling that helps us understand what we need to do better.

"You miss 100 percent of the shots you don't take."

- Wayne Gretzky

what did you learn?

"Nobody who ever gave his best regretted it."

- George Halas

my most embarrassing moment EVER!

This is how I recovered.

This is how I laugh about it now.

design your own Captain & Poet

ADVICE COLUMN

make up a letter from a fan and give them your best Captain and Poet advice! make up a fun name for them (e.g., Lost in Love or Stuck in First Gear) and yourself as well. Write back with some good advice that their Captain and Poet would give.

Use the checklist to pick a couple of themes that apply to their problems (and add a couple of your own!).

- [ ] Face your fears
- [ ] Take it one step at a time
- [ ] Do the right thing
- [ ] Trust your gut
- [ ] Be yourself
- [ ] Follow your dreams
- [ ] Look on the bright side
- [ ] Forgive and forget
- [ ] Stick to your guns
- [ ] Be the bigger person
- [ ]
- [ ]

Question

Dear ______________________,

Sincerely, ______________________

Answer

Dear

______________________,

Sincerely,

____

How do your Captain & Poet deal with the UNEXPECTED?

1. It's Halloween and you find out someone else is wearing the same costume as you.

A) You freak out and rush to figure out a new one.

B) You add some accessories to make yours more original.

C) You pretend you are them.

D) You join forces and rule the party.

2. Someone is spreading a rumor about someone you know.

A) You let your friend know and you confront the person who started it.

B) You dismiss the source and say something that proves the rumor isn't true.

C) You change the rumor so that it makes your friend look good and you pass it on.

D) You make up a positive rumor about yourself that makes you popular.

3. Your team's goalie is not feeling well and may have to back out of the game tonight.

A) You give them a bunch of vitamins and a pat on the back.

B) You call a friend who once goalie'd back in the day.

C) You suggest everyone rotates in goal.

D) You finally convince the coach to let you play defense and you save the day.

4. You realize no one in your friend group has made any plans for one of your good friend's birthdays.

A) You rally the troops and pull off a party last minute.

B) You all hop on social and bombard them with Happy Birthday messages just as the clown you ordered shows up at their house.

C) You each take a day of the week and arrange a week-long celebration!

D) You pick a random spot and time and turn it into a surprise party!

5. You get a haircut and they accidentally shave a strip of your hair.

A) You flip your hair over to the other side and buy a boatload of products to keep it there.

B) You invent a new hair style and everyone starts to copy it.

C) You announce over the P.A. System that it is national hat month and wear a hat each day.

D) You convince your parents to get you the hair extensions you always wanted.

6. You don't find out you have a test until the night before.

A) You pull an all-nighter and ace it.

B) You and a friend split the studying and then meet early the next morning to exchange notes.

C) You pin your notes to the mirror so you can study while you get ready and arrange to walk to school with a friend to quiz each other on the hard stuff.

D) You ask your crush to help you study.

7. You post the wrong photo on social and don't realize it until the next day.

A) You delete it immediately and repost what you intended to post.

B) You explain what happened and have a good laugh with everyone.

C) You invite everyone to post a silly photo to win a prize.

D) You take advantage of all the likes and comments and use the attention to promote a new YouTube channel.

→ Check Your Score! Count up the number of answers for each category:

Mostly A's

Your Captain and Poet want things done a certain way and work hard to make it happen.

Mostly B's

Your Captain and Poet are resourceful and always figure out a way to make things work.

Mostly C's

Your Captain and Poet think outside of the box.

Mostly D's

Your Captain and Poet find an opportunity in every problem.

memories of memories

The way we shape our memories creates the story of our life.

memories of special times can give us strength when things get tough. Recall a memory that reminds you of how great life can be.

Even our memories of difficult times can have a positive side to them – like what you learned or the way someone showed up for you in that time. Recall a memory that you have changed your perspective on since it happened.

How do you see the Captain and Poet in these memories?

time travel

If you could travel back in time what time period would you go to?

What would you like to experience?

What would you like to change?

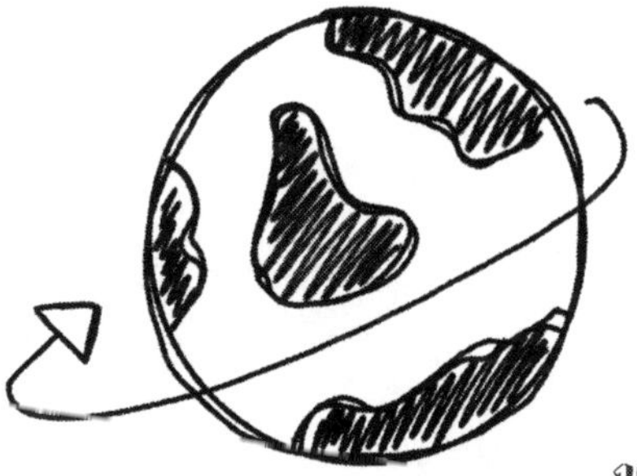

Captains & Poets on other PLANETS

What if you decided to take
a trip to another planet?

What would you hope to find?

What would you like to keep
about your life on earth?

What would you change?

Sometimes looking up at the stars helps us by reminding us that our problems are small and that we have a place in it all.

Next time you see a **SHOOTING STAR** what will you wish for?

If ANYTHING was possible I would...

spend a day in the life of...

travel to...

not do this ever again...

In 10 YEARS I will...

be living...

be hanging out with...

have travelled to...

have won...

have bought...

have finished...

have started...

In 20 YEARS I will...

be living...

be hanging out with...

have travelled to...

have won...

have bought...

have finished...

have started...

make a vision board for your best life!

(cover this up)

(but not this part)

"The vision pulls you."

– Steve Jobs

intention setting

Setting intentions is a powerful skill that brings your Captain and Poet together. The Poet helps us tune into what it is that we want to create or bring into our life. The Captain helps us move in that direction. Instead of drifting along, create your own path!

Tips for setting an intention:

1. visualizing what we want
2. Imagining how it will feel
3. Writing it down
4. Noticing how it is showing up (sometimes in ways we didn't expect)
5. Tracking our progress

We all would change the **WORLD** if we could

One thing I would change is...

This is important to my Poet because...

my Captain can help make this change happen by...

A **WORLD ISSUE** that is important to me

If you could wave a magic wand and anything was possible (because it is!), what would happen tomorrow to solve the issue?

How can you advocate for it?

what the WORLD would be like if...

... everyone was their best Captain and Poet.

... everyone saw everyone else's best Captain and Poet.

... everyone's Captain and Poet worked together.

@ CaptainsPoets GOES VIRAL

Create a message you want the world to know. Write a social media post. Make sure it is catchy!

OR

Write a blog on a topic relevant to young people like you.

OR

Pretend you are in the 20th or 19th century and write an article the way it would have been done old school! (Way more than 500 characters!)

Extra! Extra! Read all about it!

air mail

make some paper airplanes. Write an inspiring message for yourself on the wing of each plane. Randomly pick up one of the planes when you need to elevate your mood and throw it out there!

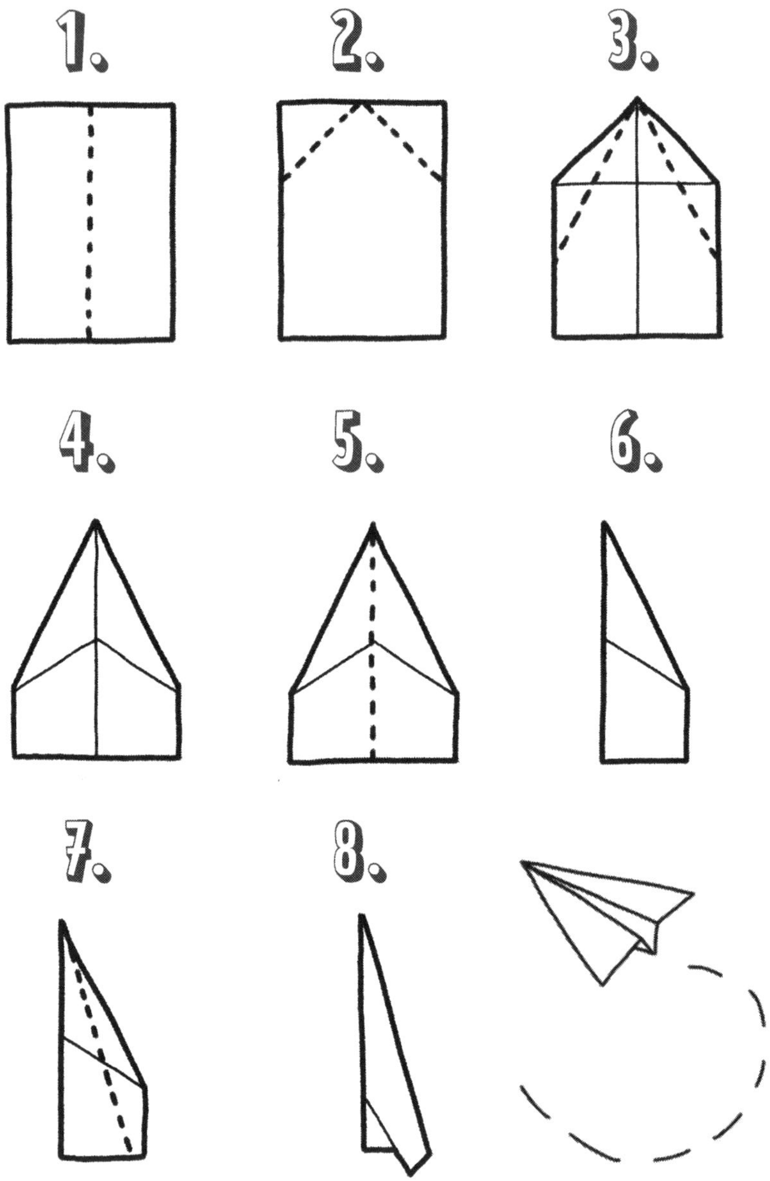

self talk

List five negative things you hear yourself say to yourself sometimes. How can you turn those into positive statements to coach yourself through tough situations?

−	+
1. my ideas are so weird.	I am creative!
2.	
3.	
4.	
5.	

unmute yourself

What do you wish you could say but can't seem to find the right words or the right timing?

Say it three different ways.

Sometimes just saying it to yourself is enough. Sometimes it isn't.

Captain & Poet yoga poses

Yoga reminds us to listen to our body and pay attention to how we are feeling. Try a few yoga poses and hold them for a little while. Remember to breathe deeply and only do what feels good. Don't forget to switch sides for Dancer, Stork and Warrior 3.

Use these poses whenever you need to get in the Captain & Poet zone.

IN A WORD

Sometimes the easiest way to explain how we are feeling is by picking one word. In a word, how are you feeling?

Try this game at the dinner table and see what you learn about everyone.

be a rebel
and colour
outside
the lines
(because nobody can be their
true self by fitting in a box!
unless you are jack of course)

a-MAZE-ing

Create a maze that represents the ups and downs and zig zags of your life.

→ Start

Finish ←

Take a PHOTO of...

Create an album on your phone and collect photos that remind you of the Captain and Poet in you and others.

...something that makes you laugh

...something that makes you happy

...something you are passionate about

...something you ___________.

text-iquette

misunderstandings aren't great but they can help us learn about ourselves and each other. Think of three rules we could all follow to help us prevent them or fix them when they happen. Your Captain and Poet know what they would do...

1.

2.

3.

TBH LOL BRB IYKYK

who do you follow ?

We follow different people for different reasons. We might find them interesting or like something about them. List the Captain and Poet qualities of the people you follow.

Find an example of Captain and Poet posts!

Captain & Poet hashtags

make up hashtags for your Captain and Poet.

#IFEELITALL

#COOLCAPTAIN

#PROMISINGPOET

#READYTOTAKEONTHEWORLD

make one that describes the unique way they each combine in you!

#ADVENTUROUSEMPATH

#HAPPYME

#BOLDCREATIVE

#ONLYQUIETONTHEOUTSIDE

They are such a Poet because...

They are such a Captain because...

favourite youtuber

me tube

Create an authentic YouTube Channel that sends your unique message and view on life out to the world.

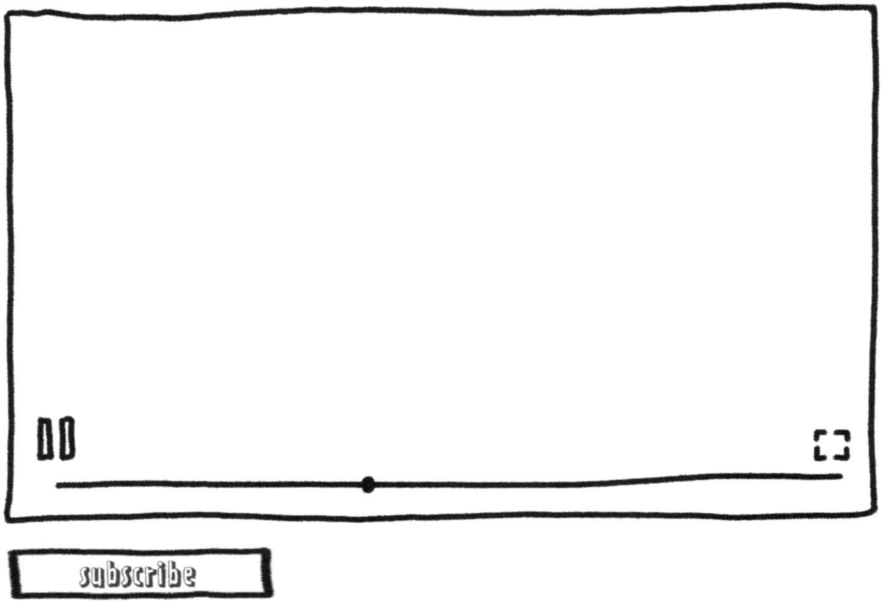

What would it be called?

What would you talk about?

What thought-provoking questions would you ask your viewers?

fictitious advice

Pick a favourite character from a book, show or movie and explain how their Captain and Poet could show up more for them. Give them some advice that would really help them.

____________________ you are such a Poet

because ____________________________

but sometimes you need to ______________

______________________________.

____________________ you are such a Captain

because ____________________________

but sometimes you need to ______________

______________________________.

If I could give you my best advice I would say

____

____

video game

Create an epic video game where Captains and Poets save the day.

make your own album cover

design your own **MOVIE POSTER**

What would the movie of your life be called?

design your own company logo

Imagine you are CEO of your own company. What is it about? What is unique about it? What difference are you making in the world?

where would you put it?

design
your own
Captain
& Poet
tattoo

Draw or design your CAR of the FUTURE

Include a bumper sticker and custom license plate! What message about Captains and Poets would you want everyone driving by you to see?

making choices

Sometimes making choices is fun, like what game to play or what to have for dessert. But sometimes choices are more serious and they can be hard to make.

Think of a choice you have to make.

Our Poet helps us know how we feel inside about each choice. How do you feel when you imagine what that choice will be like? Which choice does your Poet like the best?

Our Captain reminds us we can do anything we put our minds to and helps us to try new things. What does your Captain tell you about this choice based on your past experience?

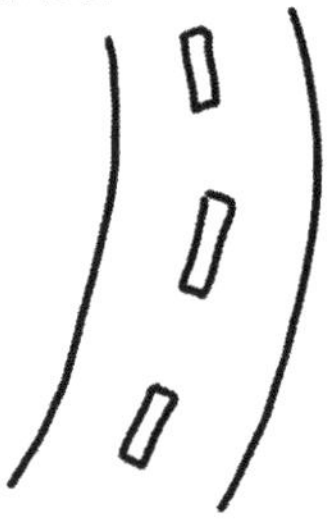

After you have made the choice, come back and tell your journal how it went! What did you learn for next time?

"Make your choices reflect your hopes, not your fears."

– Nelson Mandela

my super powers

Find the hidden phrase in the bold squares by filling the answers in for each of the clues.

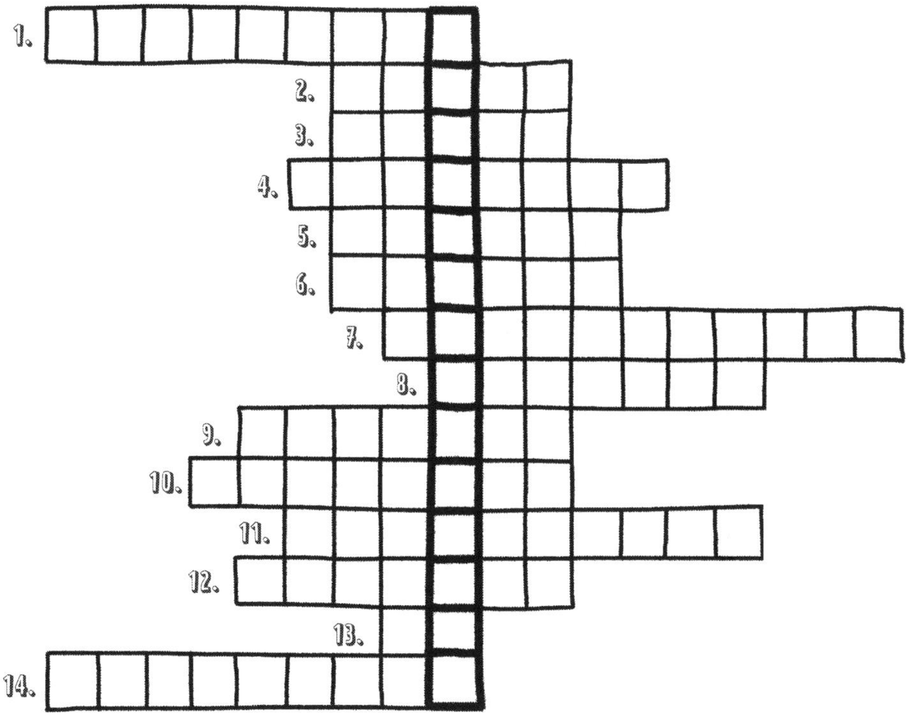

The hidden phrase is: ______________________

1. Real or genuine.
2. Feeling fear about something but doing it anyway.
3. Feeling pleasure and enjoyment in the moment
4. Expressing appreciation.
5. Someone who takes charge.
6. Special; one of a kind.
7. Something that gets your attention (the opposite of boring).
8. Extra special! Wow!
9. A special ability to do something well.
10. Kind or nice to others.
11. Feeling and showing concern for someone who is suffering.
12. Having a desire to learn or know more about something or someone.
13. The person doing this puzzle.
14. To bounce back when we have challenges.

ANSWERS: AUTHENTIC, BRAVE, HAPPY, GRATEFUL, LEADER, UNIQUE, INTERESTING, AMAZING, TALENT, FRIENDLY, COMPASSION, ME, RESILIENT

the SUPERPOWER of COMPASSION

Compassion means we care about others, treat them with kindness and feel motivated to help others in need. It connects us to others by reminding us we are all human and all have hardships to deal with.

Compassion is empathy in action. The Poet feels empathy for the person and our Captain wants to do something about it. It literally means "to suffer together".

Empathy + Action = Compassion

Think of a time you saw someone having a hard time. What did you feel? What did you do about it? If you didn't do anything at the time, what would you do if it happened again?

"Be kind, for everyone you meet is fighting a harder battle."

– Plato

! Remember, compassion is a muscle we can build over time.

Self compassion is the ability to be kind to ourselves. It is treating ourselves the way we would treat a friend or someone we love when they are having a hard time. When you have compassion for yourself you accept that you are human. No one is perfect. Everyone has a hard time sometimes. And when we are gentler with ourselves, we are better at being gentle with others.

→ **Which things do you do to show yourself compassion?**

- [ ] Give yourself a hug or pat on the back when you need it
- [ ] Be patient with yourself (Give yourself a pat on the back when you do a good job)
- [ ] Tell yourself it's okay not to be perfect (no one is!)
- [ ] Remind yourself life has ups and downs (and you will be okay)
- [ ] Remind yourself of something good about yourself when you fail or make a mistake (don't lose sight of who you are!)

→ **Now select one that you want to do more of!**

We always have our Captain and Poet to turn to.

the SUPERPOWER of GRATITUDE

Gratitude is a warm feeling that we feel towards things we are thankful for. Think of something you are thankful for right now and see if you can feel your heart get warmer. The way we feel about things can be greatly impacted by the way we look at things.

Gratitude brings our thoughts and feelings together in a powerful way. When we pay attention to life's positives, we train ourselves to see them more often. This then makes us feel more grateful! You might try feeling grateful for the weather, a friend you can be yourself with, the ability to do something that others may not be able to do, for a stranger that lent you a hand, that you made it to class on time (phew!), or that your brother or sister didn't drive you crazy today!

→ **Acknowledging these things will help you cultivate an attitude of gratitude that you can share with others.**

Name something you could be grateful for...

→ ...right now

→ ...from your childhood

→ ...something small

→ ...something big

"Just tell yourself, Duckie, you're really quite lucky!"

– Dr. Seuss

gratitude ladder

Each time we are grateful for something it builds our heart muscle to help us be even more grateful. Fill in the gratitidue ladder below. Start with something small at the bottom and see where it takes you.

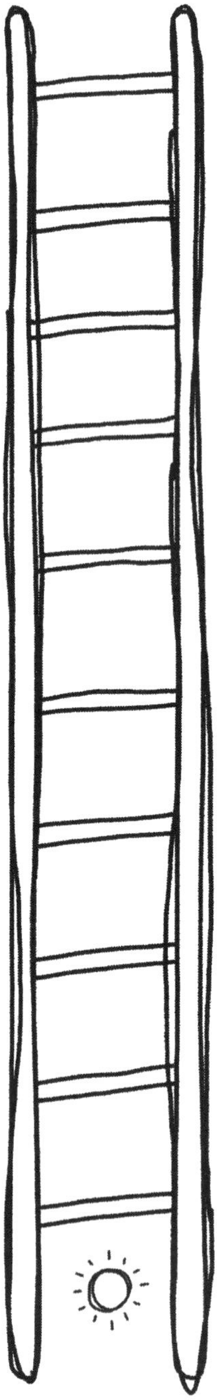

Example: I am grateful for sunshine

"I'm bored."

Have you ever heard the expression "only boring people get bored"? Think of something that bored you recently and how your Captain and Poet could help make it more interesting next time.

the SUPERPOWER of CURIOSITY

Curiosity makes life more interesting. The Poet wants to understand the world and shows its curiosity by noticing things other people don't and imagining what else there is to know. The Captain actively shows their curiosity by exploring and trying new things. Together they are great partners in curiosity. What are some of the questions that you ponder? What are some of life's puzzles you are trying to figure out?

→ **Write them down and make up a theory or answer for them.**

? Why are we so fascinated with dinosaurs anyway?

? If a tree falls in the forest when no one is there does it make a sound?

? What is love? How can we measure it?

?

?

Check off the ways you practice curiosity. Then circle Captain or Poet (or both!) depending which one you think is helping the most with that strategy.

- [ ] Asking other people's opinions on things. C OR P
- [ ] Learning new things. C OR P
- [ ] Think about how our relationship to others, things, nature, the universe, etc. C OR P
- [ ] Trying new foods. C OR P
- [ ] meeting new people. C OR P
- [ ] Learning about other cultures. C OR P
- [ ] Looking up at the stars and wondering what is out there. C OR P
- [ ] Seeking out new experiences. C OR P
- [ ] Asking questions about uncomfortable topics. C OR P
- [ ] Travelling. C OR P
- [ ] Reminding ourselves we don't know everything. C OR P
- [ ] Looking closely at things in the day-to-day that we often ignore. C OR P
- [ ] Wondering how things work. C OR P

the SUPERPOWER of RESILIENCE

Resilience is the skill of being able to bounce back from stress, failure, challenges or hard times. It is another muscle you can build and is an important tool to have to deal with life's ups and downs.

Your Poet helps you process your emotions and your Captain helps you take positive action to move forward. Both of them remind you that what you are going through isn't forever and that you will rebound.

"Our greatest glory is not in never falling – but in rising every time we fall."

– Confucious

How are trees resilient?

How is a bike resilient?

How are you resilient?

"I really think a champion is defined not by their wins, but how they can recover when they fall."

– Serena Williams

Check off the ways you practice resilience. Then circle Captain or Poet (or both!) depending which one you think is helping the most with that strategy.

- [ ] Talk about your emotions. C OR P
- [ ] Focus on what you can control (and not what you can't). C OR P
- [ ] Focus on the positive. C OR P
- [ ] Be grateful for something C OR P
- [ ] Be compassionate toward yourself C OR P
- [ ] Know that where you are is part of the journey and not the destination (you aren't stuck there forever!). C OR P
- [ ] Stay true to yourself. C OR P
- [ ] Find a way to take a small step forward C OR P
- [ ] Think of one good thing about the situation. C OR P
- [ ] Identify what you have learned. C OR P

Now circle one that you want to do more of!

the SUPERPOWER of COURAGE

"It takes courage to grow up and become who you really are."

– E.E. Cummings

On a scale of 1–10, how courageous are you:

At home

1 2 3 4 5 6 7 8 9 10

In class

1 2 3 4 5 6 7 8 9 10

In clubs

1 2 3 4 5 6 7 8 9 10

With friends

1 2 3 4 5 6 7 8 9 10

In this journal

1 2 3 4 5 6 7 8 9 10

In pursuing what you want!

1 2 3 4 5 6 7 8 9 10

→ What would happen if you were a little more courageous in one or two of those areas?

→ In which areas do you think you can get to a 10/10?

→ Consider that a year from now you may wish you had done what?

→ What step can you take to getting there?

→ What would happen if the world was full of courageous people?

"Courage is knowing what not to fear."

– Plato

confidence vs. courage

Confidence is believing you can do something and then doing it. Experience gives us confidence.

Courage is being afraid to do something and doing it anyway. Courage comes from deep inside.

Think of a situation that required you to have courage.

How did your Captain and Poet help you find the courage?

How did you gain confidence from that experience?

conquering your fears

Name something you
are afraid to do but
know that you have to.

Why are you afraid?

Write down one step
you could take toward
conquering your fear?

**"Everything you want is on
the other side of fear."**

– Jack Canfield

emotional courage

We have to be brave to share something we feel strongly about. The Poet helps us understand what we feel inside, good and bad. The Captain helps us share these emotions and do something about them. Together, they give us emotional courage! Emotional courage is not being afraid to show the world we we really are inside. When we use our emotional courage we are sharing the most important parts of ourselves.

→ Think of a time your Captain helped your Poet show emotional courage and show the world who you really are inside.

→ What was the impact on you and others?

→ What did you learn?

→ Draw a picture that shows you with emotional courage.

"Don't ask yourself what the world needs. Ask yourself what makes you come alive, and go do that...

inspired action

We have to feel something strongly to be brave. The Poet helps us know when something is important to us. The Captain helps us figure out how to take care of it. Together, they give us inspired action! Inspired action is when we feel a strong urge to do something and it won't just go away if we ignore it. And when we do it it makes us feel alive, brings us joy and helps us make our dreams come true. We know our action is inspired because it fills us with energy and makes a difference in the world.

→ Think of a time your Captain and Poet kept tugging at you to do something and it wouldn't go away.

→ How did it make a difference to you and others?

→ What did you learn?

→ Draw a picture that shows you with inspired action.

"...because what the world needs is people who have come alive."

– Howard Thurman

can you relate?

→ Name two people you know well that you can relate to and explain why. How are your Captains and Poets the same? How are they different?

1.

2.

can you relate?

Name two people you don't know well and explain how you can relate to them. How are your Captains and Poets the same? How are they different?

1.

2.

watching the WORLD go by

Spend 20 minutes on a street corner, in the mall, in a park, in a library or other public space. Notice what crosses your mind as you watch people.

What are your initial thoughts about them?

Can you find evidence of their Captain?

Can you find evidence of their Poet?

How does that make you see them differently?

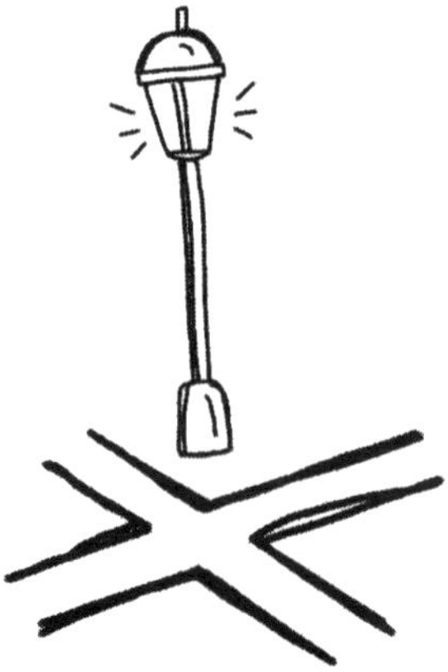

"Be curious, not judgemental."

– Walt Whitman

Can't we ALL just get along?

→ Think of someone you don't get along with.

→ What is one thing you admire about them?

→ What is one thing you share in common with them?

→ How would you describe their Captain and Poet?

→ How can you use this new understanding of them to get along better?

"A lot of different flowers make a bouquet."

– Islamic proverb

self - leadership

Self-leadership is about choosing how you show up in the world. When we are operating from self-leadership we are being our best self. Check off all the things that you do that make you a good self-leader.

- [ ] Understanding why you are choosing what you are choosing
- [ ] Operating from what is important to you
- [ ] Taking responsibility for your thoughts and feelings
- [ ] Balancing what is in your heart and in your head
- [ ] Identifying what is important to you and acting on it
- [ ] Paying attention to your intuition and what you sense
- [ ] Following your gut instincts
- [ ] Setting meaningful goals for yourself
- [ ] Guiding yourself toward good choices
- [ ] Thinking about how your actions affect you and others
- [ ] Using self-leadership to be a good leader

→ Now circle one that you want to do more of!

your true north star

We all feel a pull inside of us to go in a certain direction. This is called your True North Star. It is calling you to live the life you were meant to live.

But the world is sometimes full of noise and makes it hard to pay attention to this part of us — and then our star starts to dim. Trying to figure out your True North Star and taking action on it is part of the journey you are on.

Start paying attention to what is pulling you and the direction you are meant to go. Each time you get a glimmer of what that might be, fill in one of the points in the star and soon you will be able to see it more clearly.

Leadership

→ Who is your favourite kind of leader? What are they like?

→ How are you a good leader?

→ How does your Poet contribute to your leadership?

→ How does your Captain contribute to your leadership?

"Leadership is a choice, not a position."

– Stephen Covey

press the power button

Sometimes people try to dominate by exerting power over others or trying to be in control of things. But true or authentic power is quite different. It isn't about controlling what is going on in our external world. It is about operating from a place inside of us where we can see what everyone needs and come to a good solution.

Describe a situation where someone you know was trying to be in control or exert power over you. How did your Captain and Poet help you navigate it?

Describe a situation where you felt powerless. How could your Captain and Poet have helped you handle it in the best way for you?

Describe a situation where instead of trying to exert power and control you worked to find a solution for everyone. How did your Captain and Poet help you do this?

me?! a leader?!?

We don't realize all the ways we all lead everyday.

→ Have you ever picked up a piece of garbage on the sidewalk? (If not you, then who!?) That was leadership.

→ How do you lead in your school, family and community?

→ Have you ever had to deal with a challenging situation? That was leadership. Share what you did.

→ Have you ever made a decision for yourself or a group of people? That was leadership. What happened?

→ Have you ever questioned something that everyone else was just accepting and you knew it wasn't right? That was leadership. Share what happened.

→ Have you ever been nominated as a leader or asked to do something on behalf of a group? How did it feel to know others trust you that way?

↙ Have you ever taken care of a younger sibling? That was leadership.

Captains & Poets on the world stage

When people lead with their Captain and Poet it makes a world of difference! Think of a leader on the world stage that you admire and describe how their Captain and Poet make them so amazing.

if I ruled the WORLD...

I would...

I wouldn't...

I would work with other leaders to...

create an **avatar** of your most powerful Captain & Poet

secret code

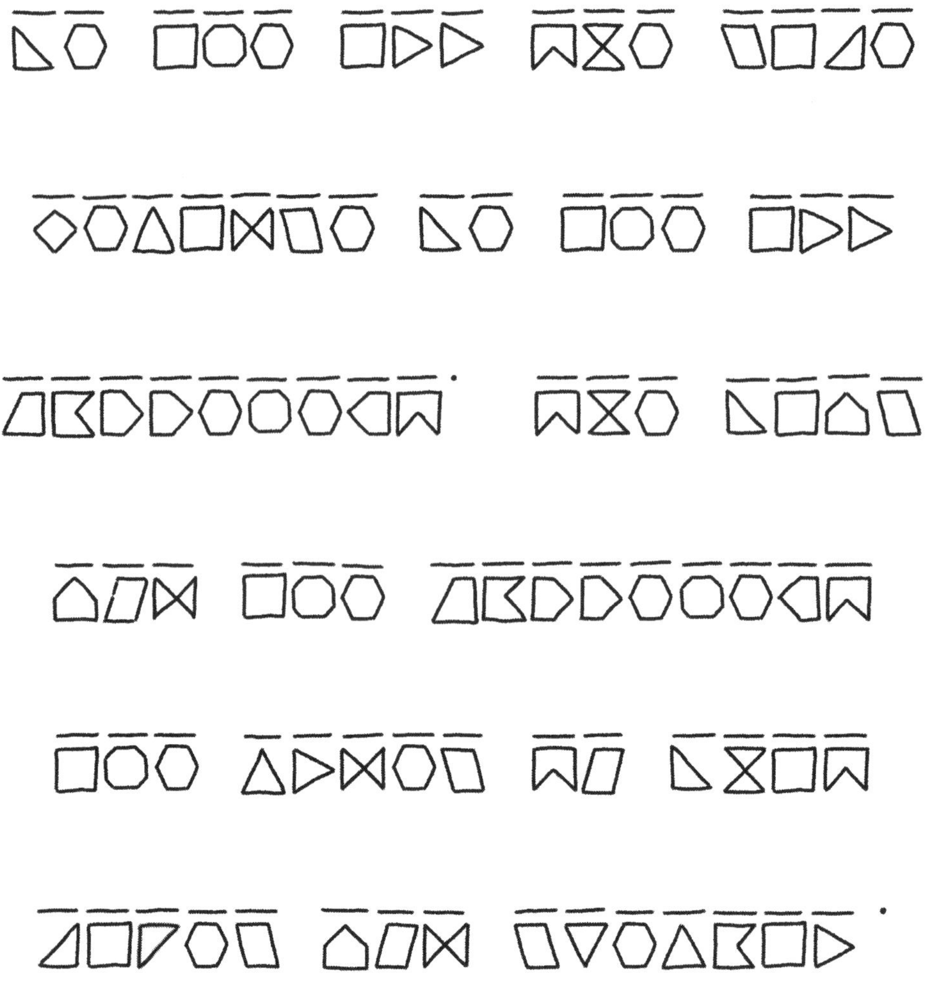

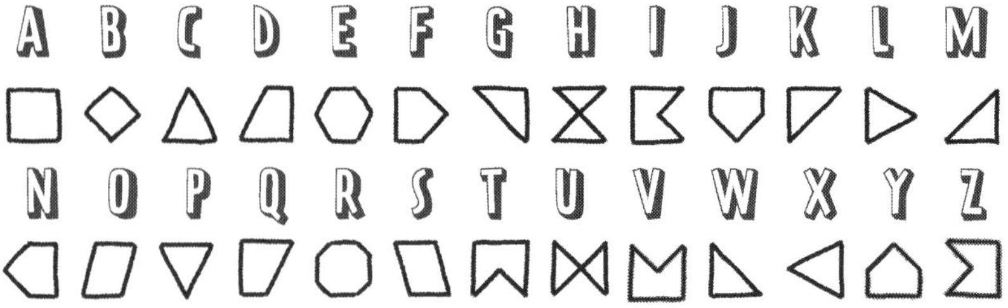

an AFFIRMATION a day keeps the blues away

Circle the affirmation that is most valuable for you today. Say it three times and repeat it throughout the day! Find an image that represents what it means to you and put it in this page as a bookmark for when you need reminding!

Every mistake I make is an opportunity to become a better human.

I need to show up for myself before I can show up for others.

I believe in my path.

I live into my dreams each day.

I have everything I need inside of me.

an AFFIRMATION a day keeps the blues away

Create an affirmation for yourself that you need to hear often. Keep it focused on the present (not the future) and put it on your mirror or fridge so you can repeat it daily!

I am...

Better Together Crossword

Down

1. The Captain and Poet remind us we are mostly the ____ on the inside.
3. When we include all parts of ourselves it is easier to appreciate and _______ others. (Because we know they have a Captain and Poet inside too.)
4. Courage comes from my _____.

Across

2. We are all the same because we are all __________.
5. Keeping my Captain and Poet in _______ helps me be my best self.
6. If everyone operated from their best Captain and Poet the world would be an _______ place.
7. By being our best self we actually help ______.

ANSWERS: HEART, SAME, BALANCE, OTHERS, AMAZING, INCLUDE, DIFFERENT

CAPTAIN & POET "QUOTES"

"Be yourself, everyone else is taken."

– Oscar Wilde

"Nobody built like you, you design yourself."

– Jay-Z

"If my mind can conceive it, if my heart can believe it, then I can achieve it."

– Muhammad Ali

"In a gentle way, you can shake the world."

– Mahatma Gandhi

"What lies behind you and what lies in front of you, pales in comparison to what lies inside of you."

– Ralph Waldo Emerson

"The privilege of a lifetime is to become who you truly are."

– Carl Jung

"Why fit in when you were born to stand out?"

– Dr. Seuss

"Follow your bliss and the universe will open doors where there were only walls."

– Joseph Campbell

"To be beautiful means to be yourself. You don't need to be accepted by others. You need to accept yourself."

– Thich Nhat Hanh

"The reward for conformity was that everyone liked you except yourself."

– Rita Mae Brown

"It is better to fail in originality than to succeed in imitation."

– Herman Melville

a quote to inspire your Captain & Poet

Pick a quote from this book (or one of your own) that means a lot to you and design a poster for it.

" "

we are all the **SAME**
because we are all **DIFFERENT**

and **DIFFERENT** is...